The Law Commission

Consultation Paper No. 120

Restitution of Payments Made Under a Mistake of Law

LONDON: HMSO

ISBN 0 11 730202 3

THE LAW COMMISSION

CONSULTATION PAPER No. 120

RESTITUTION OF PAYMENTS MADE UNDER A MISTAKE OF LAW

TABLE OF CONTENTS

A note on citations

The following works are cited hereafter by the name of the author(s) alone.

Birks, An Introduction to the Law of Restitution (paperback ed. with revisions, 1989).

Goff and Jones, The Law of Restitution (3rd ed., 1986).

Maddaugh and Mc Camus, The Law of Restitution (1990).

Palmer, Law of Restitution (1978) Vols. I-IV.

PART I: INTRODUCTION

1. SCOPE OF THE PAPER

1.1   In March 1990 the Lord Chancellor made a reference to the Commission in the following terms-

> "To examine the law relating to payments made but not lawfully due and in particular the common law rule that payments made under a mistake of law are irrecoverable, and to make recommendations."

1.2   In view of the width of these terms of reference, we think it important to make it clear at the outset the ground that we cover in this paper and on which we are now seeking the views of consultees. Save in the case of payments to and by public authorities, at this stage, we have restricted our inquiry to payments made under a mistake of law. In the case of payments to and by public authorities we consider all ultra vires payments. These are payments made to a public authority following an ultra vires demand or where the payment is otherwise not due because of a breach of public law[1] and payments made by a public authority which are either ultra vires or otherwise in breach of public law.[2]

1.3   The traditional approach of English law has been to regard payments made to another which are not legally due as generally irrecoverable and then to seek to define those particular cases in which such payments may be recovered in

---

1.   See para. 3.1 below.
2.   See para. 4.2 below.

1

a restitutionary action. Situations in which it is recognised that recovery is allowed include cases where a payment is made under duress, fraud or undue influence; where it is made as a result of a mistake of fact; or where it is made for a consideration which has failed, as where a payment is made under a contract which is invalid. Where recovery is allowed the common law mechanism has traditionally been expressed in the language of the old forms of action, here the action for money had and received.

1.4   The mere fact that a payment is made under a mistake of law is not a ground for recovery. The primary concern of this paper and the present consultation is the question of whether, and if so in what circumstances, a payment made to another as a result of a mistake of law should be recoverable for that reason. However, we also consider whether, if there is to be reform of the mistake of law rule, what defences there should be to claims for restitution on this ground.

1.5   We do not, however, propose to examine the other available grounds of recovery where a payment has been made as a result of a mistake of law. For example, a right of recovery based on the existence of fraud may be established where the relevant mistake results from the deceit of the payee but it is not proposed to consider what kind of circumstances should constitute fraud. Similarly, we do not propose to consider the availability of, for example, claims based on duress or undue influence in circumstances where there is also some mistake of law present.

1.6   Although mistake of law is the central concern of this Consultation Paper as far as it concerns private law, in the case of payments to or by public authorities, we do not only consider the mistake of law rule. It has been argued that the mere fact that making or receiving the payment is ultra vires the public authority should suffice to justify recovery of a payment made in response to a claim by or against the public authority. This approach has recently been adopted in respect of payments made to a public authority by a majority of the Court of Appeal in Woolwich Equitable Building Society v. I.R.C..[3] However, the general right of recovery was held not to extend to payments made under a mistake of law. Frequently where payments are made to a public authority there will have been a mistake of law as to whether the payment is actually due. The continued irrecoverability of payments made under a mistake of law requires consideration as the argument for the new approach is that the mere fact that the receipt is ultra vires should alone be sufficient as is the case with payments by a public authority. Thus, it has been argued that there should be recovery even where, for example, the payment is made despite a firm belief that it is not owed. It has also been suggested that whatever the basis of restitution in such cases the exceptions to or bars on recovery should be narrower than in cases of restitution based on mistake. Furthermore, a number of statutory rights to repayment have been created, some of which are simply based on the unauthorised nature of the receipt, whether or not the payment was made under a mistake of law. Since much of the criticism of the current mistake of law rule has been directed at the problem of ultra vires levies by public authorities we believe it would be unsatisfactory to consider the problem of mistake of law without also addressing these additional questions.

---

3. The Times, 27 May 1991. We understand that there is to be an appeal to the House of Lords.

1.7   Whatever the current state of the law ultimately
proves to be, we have provisionally concluded that the wider
approach to payments made to public authorities adopted in
the Woolwich case is, as a matter of policy, justified by
the special position of those authorities, the force of the
demands they may make (even if these do not amount to
duress) and the existing, piecemeal statutory developments
which provide for the recovery of certain overpayments and
ultra vires charges[4].   However, even in the public law area
we do not deal with all payments which are not due since we
do not consider payments which are not due where there has
been no breach of public law principles.

1.8   The problem of contracts made under a mistake of
law will not be considered.   In some circumstances such
contracts may be either void under the common law or
voidable in equity, because of the mistake itself or because
of some distinct ground such as illegality, and where this
is so payments made under the contract may sometimes be
recoverable in a restitutionary action.   Indirectly such
payments may be said to be made under a mistake of law in
that they are made pursuant to a contract which itself is
made under a mistake of law; but the legally relevant cause
of the payment here is the erroneous belief in the existence
of a valid contract which belief has been treated as a
mistake of fact rather than a mistake of law.   In any case,
although considerations of security of transactions are
relevant to restitutionary claims, the question of when a
mistake of law should affect the validity of a contract also
involves further considerations concerning issues such as
sanctity of contract and re-allocation of contractual risk
which we do not regard as appropriate for consideration in
this context. For similar reasons we do not consider it

---

[4].   See generally Part III.

4

appropriate to deal with the question of when, given a contract which is not legally effective for some reason other than mistake, payments made under that contract may be recoverable under the law of restitution.[5]

1.9   Finally, the discussion is confined to recovery in respect of payments; recovery in respect of services which have been rendered to another will not be considered. Our terms of reference are confined to payments and most of the difficulties have in fact arisen in respect of payments. Although some of the issues that arise where services are rendered also arise in payments cases, services cases raise additional difficulties. While a money payment is generally regarded as an incontrovertible benefit, this is not necessarily the case with services; "the identity and value of the resulting benefit to the recipient may be debatable".[6] There is also the fact that services cannot be restored: "One cleans another's shoes; what can the other do but put them on?"[7] The difficulty of restoration of services together with a principle that, as a general rule, liabilities should not be forced on people behind their backs, has meant that, in English law, recovery in respect of services has been granted in a significantly narrower class of cases than in respect of payments. These difficulties call for deeper study than we could conveniently give them in the present paper.

---

5. For this reason we do not consider the restitutionary implications of the "swaps" litigation: <u>Hazell</u> v. <u>Hammersmith and Fulham L.B.C.</u> [1991] 2 W.L.R. 372.

6. B.P. Exploration Co.(Libya) Ltd. v. <u>Hunt (No. 2)</u> [1979] 1 W.L.R. 783, 799.

7. <u>Taylor</u> v. <u>Laird</u> (1856) 25 L.J. Ex. 329, 332 (Pollock C.B.).

2. STRUCTURE OF THE PAPER

1.10   The paper is arranged as follows. The recovery of payments made under mistake of law generally, without reference to the special problem of ultra vires payments is considered in Part II. The special problems of ultra vires payments whether or not made under a mistake are examined in Parts III and IV: Part III examines payments made to public authorities and Part IV payments made by public authorities. It is convenient to divide the paper up in this way since at present there are a number of distinct rules which apply to public authorities, as well as a number of considerations which need to be addressed in order to determine the relevant principles of law applicable to them.

1.11   Parts III and IV are concerned solely with problems which arise out of ultra vires payments. What is said in Part II is generally intended to apply equally to public bodies as to private where such bodies are acting within the bounds of public law and the mistake relates to some question other than their lawful authority to make or receive a payment. Thus, if a public body makes a payment under a contract as a result of misconstruing the contract, but payment is one which it is within its lawful authority to make, we consider that the principles discussed in Part II should apply as they do to any other legal person.

1.12   The Commission is most grateful to Dr. Sue Arrowsmith, Lecturer in law at the University College of Wales, Aberystwyth, who was invited by us to prepare a draft of this Consultation Paper in collaboration with us and has made a substantial contribution to the development of this project. The views expressed, however, are those of the Commission.

PART II: GENERAL

1. THE CURRENT LAW

(a) The General Rule of No Recovery

2.1   The question whether a person may recover a payment made as a result of a mistake of law arises in a variety of contexts. A payment may be made because it is believed that there is a legal obligation to make it, but this belief turns out to be based on an erroneous view of the law and in fact no such legal obligation exists. The error may relate to a statutory obligation, as where a person pays a tax or charge to the government when no such charge is legally due. This will be considered in Part III of this paper. The error may also relate to the proper construction of a contract or a will as where an insurance contract is misconstrued and a payment is made to or by the insurance company in the mistaken belief that there is an obligation to do so. Mistakes about factors other than the existence of a legal obligation may also induce a payment. For example, a person may make a gift to a body thinking that he is entitled to tax relief in respect of the gift; but on the true interpretation of the tax laws this is not in fact the case. These are some illustrations of the kind of situation in which payments may be made under a mistake of law.

2.2   It is generally accepted that in English law the fact that a payment is made under a mistake of law is not of itself a ground for the recovery of the payment.[1] By contrast a payment made under a mistake of fact is recoverable. This is clearly so where the mistake is as to

---

[1]   Halsbury's Laws of England 4th ed. Vol. 32 para. 72; Birks, p.164.

a fact which, if true, would make the payer liable to pay[2] or where it is "fundamental"[3] and there is support for a wider test under which any mistake of fact which causes the payment creates a prima facie entitlement to recovery based on unjust enrichment.[4] Recovery is in principle possible "however careless the party paying may have been, in omitting to use due diligence to inquire into the fact."[5] The principle of recovery is qualified in a number of ways. Thus a claim may fail if:-

(a) the payer intends that the payee shall have the money at all events, whether the fact be true or false, or is deemed in law so to intend,

(b) the payment is made for good consideration, in particular if the money is paid to discharge and does discharge a debt owed to the payee (or a principal on whose behalf he is authorised to receive the payment) by the payer or by a third party by whom he is authorised to discharge the debt,

---

2. *Kelly* v. *Solari* (1841) 9 M. & W. 54; *Aiken* v. *Short* (1856) 1 H. & N. 210.

3. *Norwich Union Fire Insurance Society Ltd.* v. *Wm.H. Price Ltd* [1934] A.C. 455, 461; *Morgan* v. *Ashcroft* [1938] 1 K.B. 49. See also *Australia and New Zealand Banking Group Ltd* v. *Westpac Banking Corporation* (1988) 164 C.L.R. 662.

4. *Barclays Bank Ltd* v. *W.J. Simms Son & Cooke (Southern) Ltd* [1980] Q.B. 677, 695. Goff J.'s conclusion was based on *Colonial Bank* v. *Exchange Bank of Yarmouth, Nova Scotia* (1885) 11 App. Cas. 84; *Kleinwort Sons and Co.* v. *Dunlop Rubber Co.* (1907) 97 L.T. 263; *Kerrison* v. *Glynn, Mills, Currie & Co.* (1911) 81 L.J.K.B. 465; *R.E. Jones Ltd.* v. *Waring and Gillow Ltd.* [1926] A.C. 670.

5. *Kelly* v. *Solari* (1841) 9 M. & W. 54, 59 (Parke B.). Contrast the position in Scotland where the mistake must be "excusable"; *Taylor* v. *Wilson's Trustees* 1975 S.C. 146.

(c) the payment is made in submission to or is a compromise of an honest claim,

(d) recovery would frustrate the policy of a statutory or common law rule,

(e) the payer is estopped from alleging that he acted under a mistake of fact, or

(f) the payee has changed his position so that it would be inequitable to require him to make restitution.[6]

2.3   The modern rule concerning payments made under a mistake of law has its origins in Bilbie v. Lumley.[7] An underwriter sought to recover a sum which he had paid out on an insurance policy. The claim could have been repudiated for non-disclosure and the underwriter sought to recover the payment. He knew the relevant facts at the time he made the payment but he failed to appreciate their legal significance - a mistake of law. The matter came before Lord Ellenborough C.J., who stated that there could be no recovery of a payment made as a result of a mistake of law.

2.4   The decision was subsequently followed by the Court of Common Pleas in Brisbane v. Dacres.[8] This case

---

6. On (a) and (b), see Barclays Bank Ltd v. W.J. Simms Son & Cooke (Southern) Ltd [1980] Q.B. 677, 695, and paras. 3.62-3.63 below, on (c) see paras. 2.32, 3.62 and 3.65-3.69 below, on (d) see Morgan v. Ashcroft [1938] 1 K.B. 49; Thavorn v. Bank of Credit & Commerce International S.A. [1985] 1 Lloyd's Rep. 259, on (e) see para. 2.67 below, on (f) see Lipkin Gorman v. Karpnale Ltd. [1991] 3 W.L.R. 10 (H.L) and paras. 2.66 ff. below.

7. (1802) 2 East. 469.

8. (1813) 5 Taunt. 143.

concerned a payment made by a captain to his admiral in respect of the carriage of public treasure in the mistaken belief that part of the allowance due to the captain for this carriage was so payable. The court held that the payment could not be recovered. The judgments do not necessarily support a general rule that a payment made under a mistake of law is irrecoverable; and it is possible that the majority intended to confirm the decision in _Bilbie_ v. _Lumley_ only as an example of a narrower rule that a voluntary submission to a claim of right is binding on the payer. Goff and Jones state that "the principle in _Bilbie_ v. _Lumley_ should only preclude recovery of money which was paid in settlement of an honest claim. Any other payment made under a mistake of law should be recoverable if it would have been recoverable had the mistake been one of fact."[9] However, the approach of Lord Ellenborough was approved in _Kelly_ v. _Solari_,[10] in which the general proposition that recovery cannot be based on a mistake of law was clearly endorsed. Since then the proposition has been stated in many cases in both the public and private sectors.[11] In 1943 Croom-Johnson J. in _Sawyer and Vincent_ v. _Window Brace Ltd_[12] considered it to be "beyond argument" that a payment made as a result of a mistake of

---

9. P. 119. See also Sutton, (1966) 2 N.Z.U.L.R. 173. Goff and Jones have argued that the facts of the majority of the cases decided up to the present day, though not the dicta and the approach of the courts, are consistent with this narrower view.

10. (1841) 9 M. & W. 54.

11. The rule has also been adopted in other jurisdictions: see e.g. Palmer, p. 336 (United States); _David Securities Pty Ltd._ v. _Commonwealth Bank of Australia_ (1990) 93 A.L.R. 271, in which the Full Court of the Federal Court of Australia confirmed the rule. It was also applied in Canada until the decision of the Supreme Court of Canada in _Air Canada_ v. _British Columbia_ [1989] 1 S.C.R. 1161.

12. [1943] K.B. 32, 34.

law is generally irrecoverable, a position confirmed by the Court of Appeal in <u>Woolwich Equitable Building Society</u> v. <u>I.R.C.</u>.[13]

2.5   It has never been suggested that the general irrecoverability of payments made under a mistake of law is justifiable on grounds of principle: rather it is seen as pragmatically based. The various justifications which have been offered for the rule will be examined in detail in paragraphs 2.27-2.35 below. First, however, the qualifications and exceptions to the general principle will be considered.

(b) Exceptions and Qualifications to the General Rule

2.6   There are many qualifications and exceptions to the general rule that mistake of law is not a ground for the recovery of a payment made to another. Their basis is not always clear and it appears that some have been created in order to avoid a general rule which is seen sometimes to operate in a harsh and unfair manner.

2.7   In some of the cases where recovery is allowed in respect of a payment made under a mistake of law it is not the mistake itself which is the operative ground for relief but some other factor. For instance, payments made under duress[14] or fraud or where the payee has acted in bad

---

[13]. The Times, 27 May 1991, discussed in Part III.

[14]. Common law development, in particular concerning economic duress since 1976, has significantly increased the importance of this ground; see generally Goff and Jones, pp. 222-240.

faith may be recovered even though there is also a mistake of law. Here the duress, fraud or bad faith is a separate and distinct ground for restitution. As indicated, these cases will not be considered in this paper.

2.8   A further but more debatable ground of recovery which could operate to mitigate the consequences of the mistake of law rule, is that set out by the Privy Council in Kiriri Cotton Co. Ltd v. Dewani. The appellants sought to recover a premium which had been paid for the lease of a flat.   The payment of such a premium was illegal under legislation designed to protect tenants and an agreement to pay it was accordingly an illegal contract.   The Judicial Committee appeared to treat the matter as in principle within the mistake of law rule;   but nevertheless advised that the payment was recoverable on the ground that the parties were not "in pari delicto."   In the words of Lord Denning:[15]

> "The true proposition is that money paid under a mistake of law, by itself and without more, cannot be recovered back.... If there is something more in addition to a mistake of law - if there is something in the defendant's conduct which shows that, of the two of them, he is the one primarily responsible for the mistake - then it may be recovered back. Thus, if as between the two of them the duty of observing the law is placed on the shoulders of one rather than the other - it being imposed on him specially for the protection of the other - then they are not in pari delicto and the money can be recovered back.... Likewise, if the responsibility for the mistake lies more on the one than the other - because he has misled the other when he ought to know better - then again they are not in pari delicto and the money can be recovered back".

---

15. [1960] A.C. 192, 204.

2.9   Despite its width, the statement is generally considered to apply only to payments made contrary to a regulatory provision. The Supreme Court of Canada has applied the in pari delicto principle outside this context to the situation where a public authority levied charges which were ultra vires, the levying officer being held not to be in pari delicto with the taxpayer.[16] That application of the principle has been doubted both judicially[17] and by commentators.[18]   There seem to have been no cases in England in which it has been applied outside its original context, and its status as a general principle is thus clearly in some doubt although there is support for it to be so extended.[19]

2.10   A payment made under a mistake of law may also be recovered where there is an agreement to repay if it turns out that the money was not in fact due. The courts have also been willing to imply such an agreement where a payment is made in circumstances where there is some articulated dispute as to the existence of an alleged legal obligation to make the payment, particularly if the parties had taken steps to have the matter resolved by the courts at the time the payment was made.[20] In such a situation it might be

---

16. Eadie v. Township of Brantford [1967] S.C.R. 573.

17. Hydro Electric Commission of the Township of Nepean v. Ontario Hydro [1982] 1 S.C.R. 347 per Estey J.

18. Goff and Jones, p. 126 describe it as a "novel extension of Kiriri Cotton". Maddaugh and McCamus, p. 268 state that the doctrine was "wrenched out of its illegal contract context" in Eadie. And see Crawford, (1967) 17 U.of T.L.J. 344.

19. See Birks, p. 167.

20. Woolwich Equitable Building Society v. I.R.C. [1989] 1 W.L.R. 137; The Times, 27 May 1991 (C.A.); Sebel Products Ltd. v. Commissioners of Customs and Excise [1949] Ch. 409. These cases are discussed further in Part III.

said that there is no mistake anyway;[21] but it is possible that a mistake can be said to exist in at least some circumstances of doubt. In such a case implied agreement would permit recovery when the law of restitution does not although it should be noted that it may not be entirely satisfactory, since it does not necessarily follow from the implication of a contract to repay that it will be implied that interest is payable.[22]

2.11   This paper is not concerned specifically with these quite distinct grounds of recovery. However, it is relevant to note that a number of these grounds, to the extent that they may apply in circumstances where a payment is prompted by a mistake of law, are capable of being used by the courts in order to avoid the mistake of law rule; and it is possible to point to a number of cases in which they have been used in this way.[23]

2.12   There are also a number of other situations in which relief is given in respect of payments made as a result of a mistake of law, which may be said to be exceptions to the general rule in that mistake alone appears to be the ground for recovery, although it is a mistake of law.[24] We invite comments on whether the general rule is

---

21. In Sebel, supra at p. 413, Vaisey J. suggested that an alternative answer to the problem in the case might be that the plaintiff could not have been under a mistake as to the law in making payment at a time when it was asking the court to tell it what the law was.

22. Woolwich Equitable Building Society v. I.R.C. [1989] 1 W.L.R. 137; The Times, 27 May 1991 (C.A.).

23. e.g., Eadie v. Township of Brantford [1967] S.C.R. 573.

24. Goff and Jones, pp. 128-135; Palmer, pp.343-357.

satisfactory given the existence of these exceptions.

(i) Overpayments by Trustees and Personal Representatives

2.13   Trustees or personal representatives who make overpayments as a result of a mistake of law may obtain relief against their error in some circumstances: it is established that they may normally deduct the amount of overpayments to a beneficiary from future instalments due to that beneficiary.[25]   In proceedings brought by next of kin against persons to whom parts of an intestate's estate had wrongly been distributed, it has been held that without mistake of fact there can be no action for money had and received.[26]   However, next of kin may recover in equity from a volunteer who receives a distribution under a mistake of law provided that their remedies against the personal representatives have been exhausted.[27]   There is no

---

25.   Dibbs v. Goren (1849) 11 Beav. 483;   Re Musgrave [1916] 2 Ch. 417. See further Goff and Jones, p. 128.   In the context of overpayments of rates permitting deductions has been said to be anomalous: R. v. Tower Hamlets L.B.C., Ex p. Chetnik Developments Ltd [1988] A.C. 858, 876-7, (para. 3.11 below) and in the context of landlord and tenant such deduction of an overpayment from a later payment of rent was not permitted : Sharp Bros. & Knight v. Chant [1917] 1 K.B. 771 (C.A.).

26.   Re Diplock [1947] Ch. 716, 725-726 per Wynn-Parry J.

27.   Re Diplock [1948] Ch. 465 (C.A.), affirmed on appeal sub nom. Ministry of Health v. Simpson [1951] A.C. 251.   The decision in the House of Lords was limited to the administration of a deceased's estate as opposed to the execution of a trust: ibid. at pp. 265-6 and pp. 274-5 per Lord Simonds.   It is not clear whether the same principle would apply to enable beneficiaries under a trust to recover from a wrongly paid volunteer: see Goff and Jones, pp. 575-6; Underhill and Hayton, Law Relating to Trusts and Trustees (14th ed., 1987), pp. 366-8.

reported English case where a trustee or personal representative has himself recovered money paid under a mistake of law from the recipient although recovery is allowed in some other jurisdictions.[28]

(ii) Payments made to an Officer of the Court

2.14   Payments made under a mistake of law to an officer of the court may be recovered.   In Ex parte James[29]   a trustee in bankruptcy who had been paid by an execution creditor who mistakenly believed the trustee was entitled to the money was required to repay it.   The reasons given were that he ought to set an example to the world by paying it to the person really entitled to it and that "the Court of Bankruptcy ought to be as honest as other people".[30]   The rule does not apply to a voluntary liquidator as he is not an officer of the court.[31]   It might be thought unsatisfactory that rights in a winding up may be affected differently according to whether the winding up is compulsory or voluntary.   More fundamentally, the first reason for this exception suggests that it is somehow improper to rely on one's legal rights which puts into question, at a minimum, the ambit of the mistake of law rule.   Moreover, the second reason overlooks the fact that other people are not in fact required to return payments made as a result of such a mistake.

---

28. See Goff and Jones, pp. 128-9.

29. (1874) L.R. 9 Ch. App. 609.

30. At p. 614 per James L.J.   Re Carnac (1885) 16 Q.B.D. 308 suggests the rule is of general application.   See further Goff and Jones, pp. 129-133.

31. Re T.H. Knitwear (Wholesale) Ltd [1988] Ch. 275.

(iii)   Payments made by an Officer of the Court

2.15   It has also been held that payments made by an
officer of the court as a result of an error of law are
recoverable.   In a brief judgment it was stated that the
Court had the right to order repayment as it was its own
mistake that had caused the payments.[32]

(iv)   Mistakes of Foreign Law

2.16   Money paid under a mistake of foreign law has been
regarded as recoverable, the explanation most commonly given
for this rule being that questions of foreign law are
treated in English law as questions of fact to be proved by
evidence.[33] Although unfamiliarity with foreign law
justifies the evidential rule, it is difficult to see why,
once the foreign law has been so proved, the mistake should
continue to be regarded as one of fact for all purposes.[34]
There appears to be no convincing reason why this factor
should have any significance with respect to the question of
whether recovery should be allowed of a mistaken payment.

---

32. Re Birkbeck Permanent Benefit Building Society [1915] 1
    Ch. 91.

33. Goff and Jones, p. 134; Halsbury's Laws of England, 4th
    ed., Vol. 32 para. 9.   See also R.S.C. Order 38 r.7.
    Although there is no reported decision that establishes
    a right to recover a payment made under a mistake as to
    foreign law, the reasoning of the Court of Appeal in
    Andre & Cie S.A. v. Ets Michel Blanc & Fils [1979] 2
    Lloyd's R. 427 (misrepresentation of foreign law held to
    give rise to a right to rescind) and The "Amazonia"
    [1990] 1 Lloyd's R. 236 (mistake as to the effect of
    foreign legislation held to render an arbitration
    agreement void as made under a mistake of fact) is
    equally applicable in a restitutionary context.

34. Lord Goff, The Search for Principle, (1983) 59 Proc.
    Brit. Acad. 169, 176-7.

It leads to the result that a payment made under a mistake of foreign law is recoverable where an identical payment made under a mistake of domestic law is not.

(v) Mistakes in Equity

2.17   The general principle of non-recovery in the case of a mistake of law may be regarded as qualified by the equitable jurisdiction to grant relief from the consequences of mistake.   The general approach of equity in this context has not involved a strict application of the mistake of law rule: "in Equity the line between mistakes in law and mistakes in fact has not been so clearly and sharply drawn".[35]   One mechanism by which the strict application of the fact-law distinction has been circumvented has been through the somewhat artificial distinction created between mistakes as to the general law in respect of which the no-recovery rule is applied, and mistakes as to private rights.[36]   Although it has been argued that the "private rights" exception should also apply to common law claims,[37] the exception has not been construed so as to apply in this wider context.

2.18   But in general the courts of equity have felt able to relieve against payments made under a mistake whether of fact or of law if there is any equitable ground for so

---

35. Daniell v. Sinclair (1881) 6 App.Cas. 181, 190.

36. Cooper v. Phibbs [1867] L.R. 2 H.L. 149.   See also Earl Beauchamp v. Winn (1873) L.R. 6 H.L. 223, 234, where a distinction was drawn between ignorance of a well known rule of law and ignorance of a matter of law arising in the doubtful construction of a grant.

37. Winfield, (1943) 59 L.Q.R. 327.   See also Maddaugh & McCamus, pp.264-5.

doing. That in equity there is such flexibility in terms of the granting of relief does not mean that the discretion is unlimited and at least in one case the mistake of law rule has been given full effect.[38] Even in a court of equity relief will be denied in the case of a simple money claim where there is neither a fiduciary relationship nor any equity to intervene as a consequence of the conduct of the parties.[39] However, it has also been stated that in equity "circumstances of circumvention or fraud"[40] are not a precondition to relief from the consequences of a mistake of law.

2.19   In particular a willingness to grant relief for mistake is evident in the case of a voluntary transaction by which a party intends to confer a bounty on another. Where the transaction has been effected by deed, "the deed will be set aside if the court is satisfied that the disponor did not intend the transaction to have the effect which it did. It will be set aside for mistake whether the mistake is a mistake of law or of fact, so long as the mistake is as to the effect of the transaction itself and not merely as to its consequences or the advantages to be gained by entering into it".[41] It has recently been stated in this context that "the proposition that equity will never relieve against mistakes of law is clearly too widely stated."[42]

---

38. British Homophone Ltd v. Kunz (1935) 152 L.T. 589, in which Cooper v. Phibbs was not cited.

39. Rogers v. Ingham (1876) 3 Ch.D. 351.

40. Clifton v. Cockburn (1834) 3 My. & K. 76, 99.

41. Gibbon v. Mitchell [1990] 1 W.L.R. 1304, 1309 per Millett J.

42. Ibid.

2.20   The policy considerations underlying mistake generally also appear to apply in this context. Principally, they concern finality and security of receipts. Hence, where in equity relief is sought from the consequences of a mistake, such relief will be denied regardless of whether the mistake is construed as one of fact or law where the risk has been assumed by the parties. In the case of a mistake, either of fact or law, where there is evidence that a compromise has been entered into or a submission to an honest claim equity will not grant relief.[43]   Overall, the manner in which the discretion to grant relief in equity from the consequences of mistake has been exercised highlights the shortcomings of the strict application of the mistake of law rule and illustrates a willingness on the part of the courts not to apply the mistake of law rule where considered appropriate.

(vi)   Ultra Vires Charges and Taxes

2.21   The general no-recovery rule is also qualified in respect of ultra vires payments.[44]   In some of these cases recovery is based on the fact that payment was made as a result of mistake;   in others simply on the fact that the payment was not lawfully due.   These cases will be considered further in Parts III and IV.   It should also be noted that where a payment is levied in contravention of European Community law, Community law may require the courts to give a remedy for the return of the payment.   This is predominantly a problem of public law and as such is more usefully examined in Part III of this paper. In some cases, though, as is explained later, Community law may impose

---

43. Re Hatch [1919] 1 Ch. 351.

44. For the meaning of this see para. 1.2 above.

obligations on persons generally regarded as private bodies rather than public authorities.[45] It would seem that a private party levying a charge in breach of Community obligations would be required to return it in accordance with the usual provisions of Community law.

(c) The Distinction Between Fact and Law

2.22   The contrast between payments made under a mistake of law and those made under a mistake of fact has been noted.[46] The courts are thus required to draw a distinction between questions of law and questions of fact. This is a distinction which is required to be made in many other contexts, and which is notoriously difficult to make.[47] In any context this difficulty is likely to produce uncertainty. The uncertainty may be exacerbated by a temptation to avoid the perceived unfairness of the mistake of law rule. Examples, albeit in the context of rescission rather than restitution, are provided by Lord Westbury's distinction between mistakes as to the general law and mistakes as to private rights discussed above[48] and Solle v. Butcher.[49] In Solle v. Butcher a lease was

---

45. See para. 3.44 below.

46. See para 2.2 above.

47. See, for example, Andre & Cie S.A. v. Ets Michel Blanc & Fils [1979] 2 Lloyd's R. 427, 430 per Denning M.R. (the distinction between law and fact is very illusory and so difficult to define that it should be discarded); The "Amazonia" [1990] 1 Lloyd's R. 236, 250 per Dillon LJ (it is difficult to see any sense in drawing a distinction between matters of English law and matters of foreign law in relation to an international shipping contract).

48. See para. 2.17.

49. [1950] 1 K.B. 671. Contrast the approach in Holt v. Markham [1923] 1 K.B. 504 where, however, the

entered into under a mistaken belief that repairs and alterations to a flat meant that it would no longer be subject to the statutory standard rent. Bucknill and Denning L.JJ. held that the lease had been entered into under a mistake of fact and could be set aside. Jenkins L.J., dissenting, stated that the mistake was one of law. The parties knew all the material facts bearing on the effect of the statutes on the flat but had materially misapprehended the effect of those statutes in the circumstances. We have seen that it has been suggested that the consequences of the rule are avoided with respect to payments made under a mistake of foreign law by categorising foreign law as fact. Another way in which the fact-law distinction has been manipulated in order to achieve the desired conclusion is shown by the decision of the Supreme Court of Canada in George (Porky) Jacobs Enterprises Ltd. v. City of Regina.[50] The plaintiff had paid licence fees to the municipality at a daily rate. Both parties believed these amounts to be due under a by-law but it only required the payment of an annual fee. The court held that the plaintiff had been mistaken as to the existence of a by-law requiring the payment of the particular fees; that was a mistake of fact and hence he could recover. On this basis a payment of invalid taxes would be recoverable by any party who had not studied the actual legislation on which the demand for payment was purportedly based but had simply paid in response to a demand since it could be said that that party had made a mistake as to the existence of legislation authorising the tax.

---

49. Continued
    application of the mistake of law rule was not unfair because the payee had changed his position in reliance on the payment.

50. [1964] S.C.R. 326.

2. THE CASE FOR REFORM

(a) Arguments for Reform

2.23 The rule that payments made under a mistake of law are irrecoverable has been the subject of dissatisfaction for a long time. The courts themselves have shown a dislike for a no-recovery rule of such a general nature: this is evidenced by their creation of the many exceptions to the rule and the way in which the distinction between law and fact has been manipulated. It is also evidenced by judicial statements that it may not always be consistent with the highest standards of probity and fair dealing for a payee to rely on the general rule.[51] Reliance on it has been said to be "dishonourable"[52] and "shabby"[53] and a practice has developed under which the Crown does not rely on the mistake of law rule to avoid repayment without the Attorney General's approval. The rule has also been condemned repeatedly by commentators;[54] and its abrogation has been

---

51. Ex parte James (1874) L.R. 9 Ch. App. 609 (para 2.14 above); Sebel Products Ltd v. Commissioners of Customs and Excise [1949] Ch. 409 (para. 3.52 below).

52. Re T.H. Knitwear (Wholesale) Ltd. [1988] Ch. 275, 289 (Slade L.J.).

53. Re Carnac (1885) 16 Q.B.D. 308, 312 (Lord Esher M.R.).

54. See, e.g., Goff and Jones, Ch. 4; McCamus, "Restitutionary Recovery of Moneys Paid to a Public Authority Under a Mistake of Law: Ignorantia Juris in the Supreme Court of Canada" (1983) 17 U.B.C.L.R. 233; Knutson, "Mistake of Law Payments in Canada: A Mistaken Principle?" (1979) 10 Man. L.J. 23; Needham, "Mistaken Payments: A New Look At An Old Theme" (1978) 12 U.B.C.L.R. 159. There is also voluminous literature in the United States, much of it condemning the rule: see Palmer, p. 337. Tentative support for the rule is expressed by Birks, p. 166. See also Sutton, "Kelly v. Solari: The Justification of the Ignorantia Juris Rule" (1966) 2 N.Z.U.L.R. 173.

advocated by a number of law reform bodies.[55] No comparable rule is to be found in continental legal systems,[56] in several common law jurisdictions the rule has been substantially repealed by statute,[57] and in Canada the rule has now been judicially overturned.[58] It has been asserted that "[i]t would be difficult to identify another private law doctrine which has been so universally condemned"[59] or another reform measure which enjoys such widespread support.

2.24   The main argument for reform is that the current rule allows the payee to retain money in circumstances in which it seems unjust for him to do so as against the payer. The payee is enriched by the receipt of the payment which the mistaken payer did not intend him to have and would not have been made but for the mistake; i.e. the payment was involuntary.   In the context of mistake of fact the consequence is that the payee's enrichment is prima facie unjust and recoverable in accordance with the rules outlined

---

55. Law Reform Commission of British Columbia, Report on Benefits Conferred under a Mistake of Law, LRC 51 (1981); New South Wales Law Reform Commission, Restitution of Benefits Conferred under a Mistake of Law, LRC 53 (1987); Law Reform Committee of South Australia, Report Relating to the Recoverability of Benefits Obtained by Reason of Mistake of Law (84th Report, 1984). There appears to be no body which has recommended retention of the rule after an examination of its operation.

56. R. v. Tower Hamlets L.B.C., Ex p. Chetnik Developments Ltd.[1988] A.C. 858, 882.

57. The reforms are discussed at paras.2.45-2.54 below. The rule does not apply in India: section 72 of the Indian Contracts Act.

58. Air Canada v. British Columbia [1989] 1 S.C.R. 1161, on which see para. 2.39 below.

59. Maddaugh and McCamus, p.256.

above.[60] The same considerations apply where the mistake is of law and here too the payee should prima facie be liable to repay a "windfall" benefit which he was not intended to have.

2.25   Secondly, the present law does not treat like cases alike. Inconsistency arises from the different treatment given to mistakes of law and mistakes of fact. Thus, an insurer who pays forgetting that the premium has not been paid and the policy has lapsed, has made a mistake of fact and can recover[61] while one who pays not appreciating that facts in his knowledge or of which he had the means of knowledge would have enabled him to repudiate liability for non-disclosure has made a mistake of law and cannot.[62] Inconsistency also arises from the apparent arbitrariness of the exceptions and qualifications to the mistake of law rule so that there is inconsistency in the treatment of what are really "like" cases of mistake of law itself. The distinctions between payments made under a mistake of law in voluntary and compulsory winding up[63] and the approach of equity, in particular the distinction between mistake as to

---

60. Para. 2.2 above. Recovery might also be justified on other grounds, for example economic efficiency (see Beatson and Bishop, "Mistaken Payments in the Law of Restitution" (1986) 36 U of T.L.J. 149) but the need to prevent the unjust enrichment of the payee at the payer's expense is normally considered the primary justification for allowing recovery.

61. Kelly v. Solari (1841) 9 M. & W. 54.

62. Bilbie v. Lumley (1802) 2 East. 469 (para. 2.3 above). Contrast the approach in Solle v. Butcher [1950] 1 K.B. 671.

63. Para. 2.14 above.

B

the general law and as to private rights, exemplify this kind of inconsistency.[64]

2.26   A third argument favouring reform is the uncertainty and complexity of the present law.   The uncertainty arises for similar reasons to the inconsistency; the fineness of the fact-law distinction and the many exceptions and qualifications to the general no-recovery rule.   Uncertainty also results from the way in which other grounds of recovery - such as duress or implied contracts to repay - are open to manipulation in order to avoid the mistake of law rule.

(b)   Arguments for the Mistake of Law Rule

2.27   What then are the arguments which have been proffered in support of the rule?   In Bilbie v. Lumley Lord Ellenborough stated that:

> "Every man must be taken to be cognizant of the law;   otherwise there is no saying to what extent the excuse of ignorance might not be carried.   It would be urged in almost every case."[65]

2.28   Lord Ellenborough seems to have in mind here the Latin maxim ignorantia juris non excusat, "ignorance of the law is no excuse".   The maxim is applied in criminal law and the law of tort: a party is not able to escape civil or criminal liability for wrongful acts by pleading ignorance of the law.   However, in restitutionary claims the litigant is not seeking to avert liability for a wrongful act but simply to save himself from loss;   and public policy does

---

64. Para. 2.17 above.

65. (1802) 2 East. 469, 472.

26

not require that he be unable to raise his ignorance of the law. The maxim is generally considered irrelevant to the mistake of law rule, and has not widely been relied upon in subsequent decisions.

2.29   However, although not always articulated in the decisions themselves, concern to protect; (i) the position of the individual payee and, (ii) security of receipts and certainty more generally appear to have influenced the adoption of the no-recovery rule. Both concerns are only relevant where payees believe they are entitled to the payment or, where the payment is a submission to or a compromise of a claim, have a reasonable ground for suing in respect of the claim.[66] Even under the present law a payee who is in bad faith, which includes knowledge that the payment is made under a mistake of law,[67] may not keep the payment.

(i)   The position of the individual payee

2.30   A payee who believes the payment to be his own to do with as he will has an interest in the security of his receipt. This interest may be an "expectation" interest, that is if repayment is required, the expectations generated by the fact of the payment to him will be disappointed. Of greater concern, there is also the possibility that the payee will have relied on the receipt by making expenditure or incurring liabilities which he would not otherwise have

---

[66.] On compromises of invalid or doubtful claims, see Chitty on Contracts (26th ed., 1989), paras. 190-192. See further para. 3.66 below.

[67.] Goff and Jones, pp. 125-126; Halsbury's Laws of England 4th ed., Vol. 32, para. 74.

made, and if he were required to return the payment he would be in a worse position than if the payment had never been made. This concern was mentioned by both Mansfield C.J. and Gibbs J. in <u>Brisbane</u> v. <u>Dacres</u>.[68] However, both the expectation interest and the possibility of reliance by the payee exist in cases of payments made under a mistake of fact where there is nevertheless a prima facie right to restitution and in cases where restitution is allowed on other grounds. In those contexts it appears to have been accepted that these interests are not sufficient to justify retention of a payment, unless the conduct of the payer is such as to give rise to an estoppel. In any event the possibility that the payee will have detrimentally relied on the payment cannot justify a rule barring recovery even if there has been no such reliance.

2.31   While the possibility of reliance by the payee should not affect the formulation of the grounds for recovery, the availability of a defence specifically dealing with such reliance might well be thought to do so. English law has now recognised such a "change of position" defence in <u>Lipkin Gorman</u> v. <u>Karpnale Ltd</u>.[69] where Lord Goff acknowledged that this would enable a more generous approach to be taken to the recognition of the right to restitution, in the knowledge that the defence is, in appropriate cases, available.

2.32   The third aspect of this concern for the position of the individual payee is the policy of the law in upholding submissions to bona fide claims. Many mistakes of

---

[68]. (1813) 5 Taunt. 143.

[69]. [1991] 3 W.L.R. 10. See further paras. 2.66 ff. below.

law are made where one party pays under a mistaken belief that he is under a legal liability to make the payment. For instance, Lord Esher M.R. said that the no-recovery rule has been adopted for the purpose of putting an end to litigation; "the Court allows the [payee] to do a shabby thing in order to avoid a greater evil, in order that is, to put an end to litigation".[70] It is the law's policy that if a claim is disputed by the payer he ought to be prepared to submit to litigation to resolve the matter and that if he chooses to pay rather than resist and dispute the claim, the payee ought to be able to consider the matter settled. This policy also applies to payments made under mistakes of fact; a party may not recover a payment made in voluntary submission to an honest but erroneous claim by the payee.[71] However, the policy cannot justify a general rule that payments made under a mistake of law cannot be recovered as opposed to one precluding recovery only in cases where there is such a submission.

2.33   Finally, it should be noted that the concern with the position of an individual payee has been regarded as of particular significance in relation to payments made to public authorities, considered in part III of this paper. It is argued that to allow recovery of taxes and other charges paid under mistake of law to public authorities might seriously disrupt the finances of such authorities, although concern about disruption did not appear to influence the formulation of the general restitutionary principle in the Woolwich case.[72]   Again, however, this is

---

[70.] Re Carnac (1885) 16 Q.B.D. 308, 312.

[71.] See Andrews, "Mistaken Settlements of Disputable Claims" [1989] L.M.C.L.Q. 431.

[72.] Para. 3.57 below.

not necessarily an argument in favour of a general rule
denying recovery in all cases.

(ii) General concern with security of receipts

2.34   The second justification for the rule precluding
recovery of payments made under a mistake of law is the
security of receipts generally.   Allied to this is concern
with certainty.[73]   We are not here considering the
individual payee and the interest which he has in retaining
a specific payment but the interest of recipients of
payments generally, who will wish to be secure in the belief
of their right to dispose of such payments as they please.
Where, as in the case of public bodies, the payee receives
many payments, to allow settled matters (some long settled)
to be reopened may be disruptive to the conduct of the
payee's affairs.   Furthermore, for instance in the case of
overpaid taxes, it could not be guaranteed that all relevant
cases could be identified and unfairness in the treatment of
payers might result.   If payments made as a result of a
mistake of law are generally recoverable, it could be argued
that, since such mistakes are frequent there will often be
recovery of payments and payees generally will not be able
to rely on their receipts.   This does not, however, seem to
us to be a convincing argument.   Recovery of payments is
already allowed on grounds other than mistake of law which
do not depend on the conduct of the payee, including mistake
of fact.   Further, the addition of mistake of law as a
ground for recovery in the private sphere may not
significantly increase the number of cases in which there is
recovery, since in many cases recovery will be precluded

---

[73]. For the view that the mistake of law rule should
primarily be retained as promoting certainty, see (1931)
45 Harv. L. Rev. 336.

either because there has been a voluntary submission to an honest claim or there has been no mistake. Furthermore, the security of recipients may be adequately catered for by the defence of change of position. As far as the argument for certainty is concerned, it has been argued that the present law is uncertain and complex.[74] It is doubtful that to allow recovery on the grounds of mistake of law will significantly increase the general uncertainty.

2.35   Another aspect of concern with security of receipts is the argument that to allow recovery for mistake of law would lead to a large number of false claims. It is alleged that mistakes of law, perhaps more so than mistakes of fact, can easily be concocted to disguise, for example, a change of heart in making a gift. Apart from Lord Ellenborough's fear that mistake of law would be "urged in almost every case",[75] in Dixons v. Monkland Canal Co. Lord Brougham L.C. said that a rule permitting recovery of payments made under a mistake of law was not susceptible of principled restriction and opened an inquiry in each case into the degree to which the payer knew the law and was capable of applying it to the particular facts which the court would be unable to determine satisfactorily.[76]   These concerns, however, are arguably met by the requirement that the payer satisfies the burden of proof in showing that he was mistaken.

---

[74]. See para. 2.26 above.

[75]. (1802) 2 East. 469, 472.

[76]. (1831) 5 W. & S. 445, 450 (H.L. (Sc.)).

(c)   Evaluation of the Rule

2.36   There is a prima facie case for allowing the recovery of payments made to another as a result of a mistake of law, in the same way that recovery is currently allowed of payments made as a result of a mistake of fact. The pragmatic arguments in favour of the general rule barring recovery appear unconvincing: the concerns they reflect can be adequately dealt with in other ways. The abrogation of the general rule may in fact not have a great practical importance since in many cases of mistake of law recovery may be denied because the payment was made in submission to an honest claim. However, the present rule is certainly capable of producing injustice in individual cases and reform of the law appears desirable to ensure that in these cases justice is done.

2.37   The Commission has previously considered whether to seek a reference on this topic but concluded that although there was some evidence of practical, as opposed to theoretical, difficulty raised by the present state of the law, the need for reform was not pressing.[77] At that time it was envisaged that judicial reform might occur as the law of restitution developed. However, developments since 1981 suggest that judicial reform is unlikely: the courts have recently reaffirmed the rule.[78] In addition, recent decisions of the European Court of Justice suggest that it may not apply to cases with a European Community element as the rule may be in conflict with the requirements of Community law.[79] Finally, there has been piecemeal statutory

---

[77.] Sixteenth Annual Report, (1980/1) Law Com. No. 113, para.2.96; Seventeenth Annual Report, (1981/2) Law Com. No. 119, para.2.99.

[78.] See para. 2.40 below.

[79.] See paras. 3.39-3.46 below.

development in this area,[80] and section 24 of the Finance Act 1989 goes beyond mistake in giving a general right to recover V.A.T. payments which are not due. The statutory developments highlight the inadequacy of the common law rule. For these reasons we consider that the time is now ripe for further consideration of this subject.

3. OPTIONS FOR REFORM

2.38   Reform might be introduced judicially or by legislation.

(a) Judicial Reform

2.39   Judicial reform of the mistake of law rule appears to have been accomplished in Canada, as a result of the decision of the Supreme Court in Air Canada v. British Columbia.[81] The case concerned a claim[82] by the airline to recover taxes levied under unconstitutional legislation. It was argued that recovery should be allowed because the payments had been made as a result of a mistake of law. Recovery was in fact denied for a number of reasons specific to the particular facts and context of the case, and it was thus strictly unnecessary for the Court to determine whether there is a general right to recover a payment made as a result of a mistake of law. Four members of the panel of

---

80. For a dicussion of the statutory provisions for recovery; see paras. 3.20-3.38 below.

81. [1989] 1 S.C.R. 1161. See also Canadian Pacific Air Lines Ltd. v. British Columbia [1989] 1 S.C.R. 1133.

82. The case was concerned only with the question of whether interest should be paid: the taxes themselves had been repaid.

six who participated in the judgment,[83] however, differed from the court's previous position[84] and clearly expressed the view that such a right exists in Canadian law.

2.40   The difficulty with leaving the matter to the courts in England is that, although the mistake of law rule has been the subject of substantial concern for some considerable period of time, it is well established.[85]   As such only a decision of the House of Lords could change it and the complexity of the issues and the fact that, in certain contexts, statute has modified or changed the rule[86] might lead the House to conclude that it would be inappropriate to change the rule in the exercise of its judicial power.   Furthermore, many of the complexities arise in the context of claims against public authorities, and most of the opportunities for reconsideration of and statutory modifications to the rule have arisen in public authority cases.   In Part III we provisionally recommend that the position of public authorities be dealt with by

---

83.   Delivered by La Forest J., with whose judgment Lamer and L'Heureux Dube JJ. concurred.   Wilson J. dissented from the decision of the Court but expressed agreement with La Forest J. on the mistake of law point.   Beetz and McIntyre JJ., who formed part of the majority, express no opinion on this point.   Le Dain J. took no part in the judgment.   Maddaugh & McCamus, pp. 273-79;   Birks, Essays on Restitution (ed. Finn, 1990) pp. 170-174; Arrowsmith, (1990) 106 L.Q.R. 28.

84.   Hydro Electric Commission of the Township of Nepean v. Ontario Hydro [1982] 1 S.C.R. 347.   La Forest J. stated in the Air Canada case that the rule's existence had not been in issue in Nepean.

85.   The current rule has been approved by the Court of Appeal in National Pari-Mutuel Association Ltd. v. R (1930) 47 T.L.R. 110; R v. Richmond upon Thames L.B.C., Ex p. Stubbs, (1989) 87 L.G.R. 637.   See also Avon County Council v. Howlett [1983] 1 W.L.R. 605; Woolwich Equitable Building Society v. I.R.C. [1989] 1 W.L.R. 137; The Times, 27 May 1991 (C.A.).

legislation. If so, if there is also to be reform in the private sector, it would seem preferable that it be by legislation.

(b) Legislative Reform

2.41   There appear to us to be three possible approaches to legislative reform.   One is to enact a statutory rule which expressly gives a right to recover payments made under a mistake of law.   A second is to repeal the general bar against recovery whilst at the same time directing the courts to have regard to the principles which apply to mistake of fact cases in deciding whether to allow recovery for mistake of law.   Thirdly, the existing general bar on recovery could simply be removed and the courts could be left to develop the principles of recovery in its absence.

(i) A Statutory Principle of Recovery

2.42   This approach has not found favour in any other jurisdiction.   Its main disadvantage is that it requires the legislature to contemplate and resolve a number of ancillary matters relating to recovery.   There are many questions which have still to be resolved by the common law in relation to the mistake of fact rule; for example, questions relating to the availability and scope of defences, the definition of mistake, and the nature of the mistake.[87]

---

86. See generally the discussion in Pt III.   See also the statements as to the effect of statutory intervention on common law development in Murphy v. Brentwood D.C. [1990] 3 W.L.R. 414, 419, 433, 441, 451, 457.

87. See paras. 2.2 above , 3.62-3.86 below.

2.43   Although some of these issues could usefully be
dealt with by legislation others might be better left to the
courts to be resolved on a case by case basis. Candidates
for judicial development would include the definition of
mistake, the question of what constitutes a submission to an
honest claim and the parameters of the defence of change of
position.

2.44   However, other issues which might be thought best
left to the courts for determination on a case by case basis
appear to pose more difficulties. These include the gravity
or nature of the mistake, the treatment of payments made in
the mistaken belief that a debt is not statute barred, and
the effect of fault on the part of either the payee or the
payer on the right of recovery. In addition problems which
have not yet been anticipated by the courts might arise,
particularly as there has been limited opportunity for
judicial development of the law in this area.   These
problems suggest that it might be unwise to attempt a
legislative statement of the principle or principles
governing recovery for mistake of law.

(ii)   Reform By Analogy with the Mistake of Fact Rule

2.45   Secondly, legislation could apply the common law
principles governing mistake of fact to mistakes of law.
Certain basic principles could be established by legislation
while leaving the detailed requirements for recovery to be
developed by the courts.   Within this framework there are
several different ways of proceeding.

2.46   First there is the New Zealand model[88] which has been adopted in Western Australia[89] and recommended in South Australia.[90]   Section 94A(1) of the New Zealand Judicature Amendment Act 1958 provides:

> "Subject to the provisions of this section, where relief in respect of any payment that has been made under mistake is sought in any Court, whether in an action or other proceeding or by way of defence, set off, counterclaim, or otherwise, and that relief could be granted if the mistake was wholly one of fact, that relief shall not be denied by reason only that the mistake is one of law whether or not it is in any degree also one of fact."

2.47   This approach appears intended to make it a precondition of recovery that relief would have been granted if the mistake had been one of fact.   Thus, if relief would have been refused had the mistake been one of fact,[91] for example, because the mistake was not sufficiently serious, because some defence exists, or because there has been a voluntary submission to an honest claim, relief will be refused.   The model seeks to implement a prima facie right of recovery for mistake of law which contains all the

---

[88]. The New Zealand legislation is discussed, e.g., by Cameron, "Payments Made Under Mistake" (1959) 35 N.Z.L.J. 4;   Lange, "Statutory Reform of the Law of Mistake" (1980) 18 O.H.L.J. 428; and in the reports of the other law reform bodies, cited para. 2.23 above.

[89]. Law Reform (Property, Perpetuities, and Succession) Act, 1962, s.23(1).   This provision is identical in terms to the equivalent provision in the New Zealand legislation. Other aspects of the Western Australia reforms are modelled on those of New Zealand although not identical: see further the section below on reform of specific issues.

[90]. Law Reform Committee of South Australia, Report Relating to the Irrecoverability of Benefits Obtained by Reason of Mistake of Law (84th Report, 1984).

[91]. See para. 2.2 above.

limitations and qualifications which the courts have developed in relation to mistake of fact, and also to leave future development of these in the hands of the courts, except where the legislation expressly provides otherwise. This technique of linking recovery for mistake of law to recovery for mistake of fact provides a useful way to reform the mistake of law rule without a general legislative statement of the principles of recovery.

2.48   The appropriateness of the New Zealand model should be assessed against the arguments advanced in favour of reform of the mistake of law rule. One such argument is that the rule is premised on an anachronistic distinction between mistakes of fact and mistakes of law which does not address the question of whether it is unjust for the payee to retain the enrichment.   Another argument is that rather than being a rule that is applied systematically, its effect is circumvented by numerous exceptions and judicial creativity which leads to uncertainty in this area of the law.

2.49   It has been argued that the New Zealand provision does not necessarily remove the distinction between law and fact nor give rise to a right of recovery in the case of a mistake that is not one of fact.[92] Section 94A(1) simply directs the courts not to refuse relief by reason only of the fact that the mistake is one of law.   The effect of this may only be to prevent reliance on a general no-recovery

---

[92.] Law Reform Commission of British Columbia, Report on Benefits Conferred under a Mistake of Law, LRC 51 (1981) p.68.   See further Lange, op cit, and the interpretation of the legislative provisions discussed in paras. 2.53-2.54 below.   See also the discussion of William Whiteley Ltd. v. R. (1909) 101 L.T. 741 by Ralph Gibson L.J. in Woolwich Equitable Building Society v. I.R.C. The Times, 27 May 1991.

rule as a basis for refusing recovery. While the recoverability of the payment had the mistake been one of fact is thus necessary, it may not be sufficient. The Law Reform Commission of British Columbia[93] considered that under the New Zealand statute:

> "it is open to the court to decline to grant relief having due regard to the actual character of the mistake. The court need not ignore the fact that a case turns on a mistake of law. Instead it may take that into account in determining whether it is appropriate to grant relief in the circumstances of the case."

It believed that this was a desirable state of affairs and its proposals, unlike the New Zealand legislation, makes it clear that while recovery for mistake of law is to be by analogy to that for mistake of fact, and to be governed by similar principles, that recovery would have been granted had the mistake been one of fact was neither a necessary nor a sufficient condition for relief in respect of mistake of law.[94]

2.50   It would be possible to combine the features of these two approaches. Thus, it could be provided that the court shall generally have regard to the principles governing mistake of fact cases (as is done in the British Columbia proposals) and, more specifically, that it shall be a precondition for such recoverability in a case of mistake of law that recovery would be allowed had the mistake been one of fact (as is done in the New Zealand statute). If it is considered desirable to leave open the possibility that the fact-law distinction should have some significance it would seem best to provide that the court has regard to the

---

93. Ibid, p. 68.

94. Ibid, p. 82.

mistake of fact principles in exercising what would in effect be a statutory discretion given in respect of payments made under a mistake of law.

2.51   The above methods of reform, then, provide that the rules governing mistake of fact are to be a guideline for determining cases involving mistakes of law; but the possibility is retained that in some circumstances the position may differ according to whether the mistake is one of fact or law.   An alternative option would be to direct that in a case of payment under a mistake of law recovery should be allowed in every case where it would have been had the mistake been one of fact.   The choice between the two approaches depends on whether there are any circumstances in which it might still be appropriate to grant recovery for mistake of fact but not to grant recovery in parallel circumstances where there is a mistake of law.

2.52   We find it difficult to envisage a situation in which it would be appropriate to grant recovery for mistake of fact but not to grant recovery in parallel circumstances where there is a mistake of law.   It has already been explained that any fact-law distinction brings problems of uncertainty and also appears unfair.   This suggests that the best approach to reform might be completely to abolish the distinction between mistake of law and mistake of fact in the context of restitution for mistaken payments.   The Law Reform Committee of South Australia favoured this approach and recommended that the position regarding mistake of law should be assimilated to that which applies to mistake of fact.[95]   It is our provisional view that this is the most

---

95.   84th Report (1984) pp. 29-30, 32.   The Committee recommended the enactment of a provision that relief for mistake should "not be denied by reason that the mistake is one of law" (i.e. identical to the New

promising approach to reform.

(iii)   Simple Abrogation of the No-Recovery Rule

2.53   A third approach to reform is simply to repeal the general no-recovery rule created by the courts and to leave them to fashion a new recovery rule from scratch, without any specific reference to the mistake of fact rules.[96] This is the approach which has been adopted in New York and for the recovery of overpaid excise duty and car tax in the United Kingdom.[97]   Section 3005 of the New York Civil Code provides:

> "When relief against a mistake is sought in an action or by way of defence or counterclaim, relief shall not be denied merely because the mistake is one of law rather than one of fact."

Section 29 of the Finance Act 1989 provides in part:

> "(1) This section applies to proceedings for restitution of an amount paid to the Commissioners of Customs and Excise by way of excise duty or car tax.
>
> (2) Proceedings to which this section applies shall not be dismissed by reason only of the fact that the amount was paid by reason of a mistake of law."

2.54   These provisions are similar to the New Zealand legislation in that the general rule that there may be no

---

95. Continued
    Zealand legislation save for the omission of the word "only").

96. On which see para. 2.2 above.

97. For a number of legislative techniques used in the U.K., see paragraphs 3.20-3.37 below.

recovery for mistake of law is abrogated; but it may be possible to draw a distinction between mistake of fact and law where this is considered appropriate.[98]   Unlike the New Zealand legislation, however, or the proposals put forward by the British Columbia Commission, no mention is made of the rules governing mistake of fact and so there may be more room for doubt as to whether the rules are assimilated or not.   Section 29 appears to be intended to provide for recovery in the case of payments made under a mistake of law on the same basis as is provided by the common law for payments made under a mistake of fact.   However, while subsection (1) presupposes the existence of a ground for restitution, subsection (2) does not positively make mistake of law such a ground.   At present the relevant common law ground for restitution is "mistake of fact" rather than "mistake" generally and, although a court would strive to give effect to the section by finding that "mistake" is the ground for recovery, if it did not the section would not achieve its purpose.   Proceedings could be dismissed because no ground for restitution would exist.

Summary of Provisional Recommendations on the Strategy for Reform

2.55   In summary, our provisional conclusions as to the appropriate method of legislative reform are: (a) a statutory principle of recovery should not be introduced because of the inherent difficulty of anticipating in advance all the circumstances which the legislation must cover, (b) the present rule should not simply be abrogated leaving the question of the possible relevance of the present fact-law distinction entirely open, but,

---

[98]. Mercury Machine Importing Corp. v. City of New York 165 N.Y.S. 2d 517 (1957).

(c)legislation should seek to assimilate the position of payments made under mistakes of fact and those made under mistakes of law. We invite the views of consultees on this matter, in particular on the question of whether there should be any remaining distinction between the principles governing restitution of payments made under mistakes of law and those governing restitution of payment made under mistakes of fact.

4. SPECIFIC ASPECTS OF THE LAW

2.56   Although we believe that there are disadvantages in attempting a comprehensive statement of the law on mistaken payments, the impact of reform on specific areas should be considered.   If the mistake of law rule is reformed any problems in the existing law of restitution for mistake may take on a greater significance.   In other jurisdictions where the mistake of law rule has been reformed legislation has sometimes also dealt with certain issues, even though in most respects development has been left to the courts.   It is proposed to consider two areas in which it might be thought that some statutory reform could usefully be made. However, we would welcome suggestions from consultees who feel that there are other issues relevant to the law of restitution for mistake which may warrant statutory reform, but which have not been included in this paper.

(a)   Change in the Understanding of the Law.

2.57   One question is the effect of a judicial alteration of the law.   Where the general understanding of the law changes as a result of a court decision should a payment made on the basis of the former understanding of the law be recoverable?   Where the law is changed by legislation it would seem beyond doubt that a payment made on the basis of

43

the old law cannot be recovered on the basis of mistake because there is no mistake of law at the time the payment was made: at that time the law was indeed as the payer believed it to be. It seems clear to us that as a matter of policy the result should be no different where the law is effectively changed by judicial decision rather than legislation.

2.58   It can however, be argued that a payment made before a judicial "change" of the law is indeed made as a result of a mistake and therefore should be recoverable because of the commonly accepted theory of the operation of the common law that judicial decisions are declaratory and do not change the law. We believe that this would not be a desirable result: to interpret the impact of the common law in this manner is a mere fiction and should not be allowed to affect substantive rights.   In the context of income tax and inheritance tax this may well be the reason that special provisions have long been enacted to limit recovery of overpaid tax.[99] The New Zealand and Western Australia legislation have identical provisions intended to make it clear that recovery should not be allowed in such a case. The Law Reform Committee of New South Wales has recommended a similar provision.

2.59   Section 94A(2) of the New Zealand Judicature Amendment Act 1958 provides:[100]

> "Nothing in this section shall enable relief to be given
> in respect of any payment made at a time when the law
> requires or allows, or is commonly understood to require
> or allow, the payment to be made or enforced, by reason
> only that the law is subsequently changed or shown not

---

99.   See paras. 3.25, 3.27 below.

100.   The Western Australian provision is section 23 of
          the Law Reform (Property, Perpetuities, and
          Succession) Act 1962.

to have been as it was commonly understood to be at the
time of the payment."

It is the reference in section 94A(2) to the "common
understanding" of the law which seems designed to cover the
case where the law is declared by a judicial decision to be
otherwise than it was previously considered to be.[101]
However, the concept of a "common understanding" of the law
gives rise to a number of difficulties.

2.60   First, there is the width of the provision.   By
using the notion of "common understanding" it appears to
apply to all situations where there was previously a common
error as to what was, in fact, clearly the law.   This
provision goes further than is necessary to deal with the
fiction that judicial decisions do not change the law: since
there is clearly a mistake by the payer in such cases.[102]
The only objection to recovery is that to allow it might
open the door to a large number of claims; but it has
already been argued that in itself this is not a good
argument for refusing a claim.[103]

2.61   The section may also unduly limit the factors which
might be taken into account in deciding what amounts to an

---

101.   If it were to be accepted that judicial decisions
        do change the law the reference to a change in the
        common understanding of the law (as opposed to
        actual change) would be unnecessary.

102.   See the Law Reform Commission of British Columbia,
        LRC No. 51, pp. 70-72.

103.   Paras. 2.34-2.35 above, although, in respect of
        payments to public bodies, see paras. 3.70-3.75
        below.

effective judicial change in the law. It allows consideration of only the common understanding of persons. This is of course quite wide and could include the views of courts, practising lawyers and commentators, as well as those involved in and affected by the relevant legal rules, but might be thought to preclude consideration, for example, of the particular court's own view of the weight of authority.[104] It would seem desirable that the court should be able to determine the question of whether a decision constitutes an effective judicial "change" in the law from an examination of all the evidence, and without being restricted in any way.

2.62   Because of the difficulties perceived with the application of the New Zealand and Western Australian legislation the Law Reform Commission of New South Wales recommended a rather different provision. This states that "a person is not mistaken as to the law only because, after a benefit is conferred, the law is changed."[105]

2.63   The New South Wales Commission considered that the rule should be laid down by reference to the "objective" fact of whether the law had actually changed, rather than the subjective test of the understanding of individual persons. However, this formulation begs the whole question of whether a judicial departure from a previous line of

---

104.   The question was considered in relation to the Western Australia legislation in Bell Bros Pty Ltd v. Shire of Serpentine - Jarrahdale [1969] W.A.R. 155 by the Full Court of the Supreme Court of Western Australia. In the High Court of Australia, (1969) 121 C.L.R. 137 it was not necessary to consider this point since the plaintiff's claim succeeded on another ground.

105.   See p.77, draft Bill, clause 8.

authority does actually change the law and leaves open the argument that the later decision is merely declaratory so that there has been no change in the law and the payment was therefore made under a mistake.

2.64   The difficulties with the New Zealand provision and in formulating an alternative provision to deal with this problem led the Law Reform Commission of British Columbia and the Law Reform Committee of South Australia,[106] after careful consideration, not to recommend statutory provisions on this issue.

2.65   In England the indication is that our courts would not wish to allow recovery in a case of this kind in any event.   The question was alluded to in **Henderson** v. **Folkestone Waterworks Co**.[107]   The case concerned a sum paid by way of tax which was thought at the time of payment to be lawfully due; but the contrary was later held to be the case by the House of Lords.   It was held that the payment could not be recovered.   One reason given, by both Lord Coleridge C.J. and A.L. Smith J., was that the payment was "voluntary".   This is a term often used to justify the irrecoverability of a payment even though it may have been made under some legally insufficient mistake.[108]   But the primary reason given by Lord Coleridge seems to hinge on the idea that there was no mistake of law: "at the time the money was paid...the law was in favour of the company".   This view does not sit comfortably with the declaratory

---

106.   LRC 51, (1981), p.72 (British Columbia); 84th Report (1984) pp. 30-31 (South Australia).

107.   (1885) 1 T.L.R. 329.

108.   Morgan v Ashcroft [1938] 1 K.B. 49, 66 per Greene M.R.

theory of the effect of judicial decisions but it is unclear whether the courts today would also hold that there was no mistake of law in the circumstances.[109] We would welcome the views of consultees as to how to deal with these situations and our belief that recovery would not be desirable.

(b)   The Defence of Change of Position

(i)   The Current English law

2.66   Perhaps the most important specific issue to address if there is to be reform of the mistake of law rule is its relationship with the defence of "change of position". It has been seen that one of the arguments against allowing recovery of payments made as a result of a mistake of law is that this would be unfair to a payee who has relied on the receipt, or whose circumstances have otherwise changed for the worse as a result of it. It has been suggested that this consideration does not justify a general bar on recovery. The question arises, however, as to whether a defence should be available to preclude recovery of all or part of the payment where to require the defendant to return the payment would leave him in a worse position than if it had never been made. Such a defence has been recognised in many United States jurisdictions[110] and in Canada[111] and it seems that it is now well on the way to

---

109.   Cf. Derrick v. Williams [1939] 2 All E.R. 559.

110.   See the American Law Institute, Restatement of the Law of Restitution (1937) para. 142 for a definition. See generally Palmer, para. 16.8.

111.   Rural Municipality of Storthoaks v. Mobil Oil Canada Ltd [1976] 2 S.C.R. 147.

being judicially recognised in Australia.[112]   In addition
New Zealand and Western Australia have enacted a statutory
defence of this kind applicable to all restitutionary claims
based on mistake.[113]   In Lipkin Gorman v. Karpnale Ltd.[114]
the House of Lords held that English law recognised that a
claim to restitution based on unjust enrichment may be met
by the defence that the defendant has changed his position
in good faith.

2.67   Prior to this decision the defence had received
recognition in two rather limited cases.   The first is where
an agent who has received a payment on behalf of his
principal has paid it over to the principal.[115]   Secondly,
recovery may also be precluded in certain circumstances
where money has been paid over by the plaintiff on a forged
bill of exchange and the defendant has changed his position
following receipt.[116]   A general defence was, moreover,
inconsistent with several decisions including that of the
Court of Appeal in Baylis v. Bishop of London.[117]   Apart
from these limited cases, a payee who acted in reliance on

---

112.   Commercial Bank of Australia Ltd. v. Younis [1979]
        1 N.S.W.L.R. 444; Australia and New Zealand
        Banking Group Ltd. v. Westpac Banking Corporation
        (1988) 164 C.L.R. 662.   The New South Wales Report
        (LRC 53 (1987), pp. 60-61), on the basis of the
        former case, expressed sufficient confidence in the
        likely acceptance of the defence by the courts to
        consider legislation unnecessary.

113.   See paras. 2.74-2.77 below.

114.   [1991] 3 W.L.R. 10.

115.   See Goff & Jones, pp.707-711; Birks, [1989]
        L.M.C.L.Q. 296; Burrows, (1990) 106 L.Q.R. 20;
        Millett, (1991) 107 L.Q.R. 71, 76-80.

116.   Goff and Jones, pp. 711-715.

117.   [1913] 1 Ch. 127.

the receipt of a payment had only the defence of estoppel which is available only where the payer was in breach of a duty to give accurate information to the payee[118] or has made a representation to him which has been relied on.[119]

2.68   In _Lipkin Gorman_ v. _Karpnale Ltd_. a firm of solicitors had a restitutionary claim against a gaming club for sums stolen from it by a thief and lost to the club over a period of time in the course of gaming. The House of Lords held that the solicitors could recover only the club's net receipts, i.e. less any sums paid to the thief in winnings. The House took a broad approach, considering the club's overall position rather than its position after each individual bet. The defence has most commonly been considered in the context of mistaken payments but the facts of _Lipkin Gorman_ and the statements of their Lordships show that it is not so confined and is one of the general principles of the law of restitution.[120] While acknowledging the defence for the first time the House declined to define its scope in abstract terms, preferring

---

118.   The Deutsche Bank (London Agency) v. _Beriro & Co_ (1895) 1 Com. Cas. 123, 128; _R.E. Jones Ltd_. v. _Waring & Gillow Ltd_. [1926] A.C. 670.

119.   _Avon County Council_ v. _Howlett_ [1983] 1 W.L.R. 605 (C.A.).   There was however, comment (609, 610, 611-612, 624-625) on the possible injustice of estoppel operating as a complete defence and an indication that there may be circumstances which would render it unconscionable for the payee to retain a balance of the payment.   See Davies, (1984) 4 O.J.J.L.S. 144-7; Burrows, (1984) 100 L.Q.R. 31, 34-35.   Cf Beatson and Bishop, (1986) 36 U. of T.L.J. 149, 180-1.

120.   See also _R_. v. _Tower Hamlets L.B.C. Ex p. Chetnik Developments Ltd_. [1988] A.C. 858, 882; Maddaugh and McCamus, pp. 56-7; Needham, (1978) 12 U.B.C.L.R. 159, 204.

to allow the law to develop on a case by case basis. Lord Goff[121] said that:

> "the defence is available to a person whose position has so changed that it would be inequitable in all the circumstances to require him to make restitution, or alternatively to make restitution in full. I wish to stress however that the mere fact that the defendant has spent the money, in whole or in part, does not of itself render it inequitable that he should be called upon to repay, because the expenditure might in any event have been incurred by him in the ordinary course of things."

2.69   In principle the recovery of money paid as a result of a mistake in a restitutionary action should be based on the unjust enrichment of the payee. Consequently, any available defences should similarly be based on the extent of any enrichment and the recognition of the broadly formulated defence is to be welcomed. Where a party has relied on a payment made to him which he has received in good faith he should not prima facie be required to return it: the loss ought to lie where it falls, on the payer who has initiated the loss causing event - at least where neither party is at fault. It can also be argued that such a policy promotes the general public interest in the security of receipts, allowing payees to use their receipts freely without fear of loss.

(ii)   Possible problems

2.70   The question is, however, whether the current position is satisfactory or whether it leaves the law insufficiently certain. The defence could develop in several possible ways, some of which contain disadvantages. First, the consideration of the relative fault of the

---

121.   [1991] 3 W.L.R. 10, 35.

parties and the reasonableness of the payee's conduct which
is a feature of the defence in several jurisdictions may
lead to uncertainty. Secondly, there are differences as to
what kind of reliance is required. Thirdly, broadening the
scope of recovery but making it subject to such a defence
may leave a meritorious defendant in an unsatisfactory
position because the defence can be difficult to establish.

2.71   A key issue is the exact meaning of change of
position: what changes of circumstances by the defendant
will suffice? In Canada the Supreme Court has taken a
narrow view of this and has held that specific items of
expenditure must be proved to have resulted from specific
receipts: it is not enough to show that general expenditure
has increased in line with income.[122] This approach appears
to us to exclude deserving cases from the ambit of the
defence, such as where an employer erroneously pays a sick
employee his full salary instead of the reduced sick pay to
which he is entitled and the employee simply fails to adjust
his outgoings in the light of his new income, or expenditure
which it is difficult to characterise as unusual, such as
buying "a better cut of meat, maybe, from time to time, or
something extra from the grocer",[123] and where a person with
a complicated pattern of expenditure cannot attribute any
particular items to the payment.[124] As stated by Slade
L.J.,[125] the task of having subsequently to recall and

---

122.   Rural Municipality of Storthoaks v. Mobil Oil
         Canada Ltd. [1976] 2 S.C.R. 147.

123.   Avon County Council v. Howlett [1981] I.R.L.R. 447,
         449-450 (Sheldon J.). This sufficed to raise an
         estoppel; [1983] 1 W.L.R. 605.

124.   See Law Reform Commission of British Columbia, LRC
         51 (1981), pp. 74-76; Needham, (1978) 12 U.B.C.L.R.
         159.

125.   Avon County Council v. Howlett [1983] 1 W.L.R. 605,
         622.

identify retrospectively in complete detail alterations to one's general mode of living, commitments undertaken and other transactions entered into is a difficult task. The difficulties of determining the exact extent of the loss suffered by the defendant as a result of the payment are avoided when the defence of estoppel applies since it normally precludes recovery altogether. It is, however, possible that the broad approach adopted by the House of Lords in Lipkin Gorman v. Karpnale Ltd. may deal with the type of cases referred to above. Another question concerns the way in which the court should deal with expenditure made in reliance on the receipt which takes the form of improvements to land or other property. The payee may not be able to repay without selling the improved property. In principle the factual complexities of a particular situation or difficulties of proof should not be conclusive when set against the arguments in favour of the defence. However, such considerations may affect the precise formulation of the defence and suggest that any statutory reform of the mistake of law rule should clarify the position.

2.72   It is also necessary to consider the effect of the relative fault of the parties in failing to avoid the mistaken payment (which is taken account of by the Restatement of Restitution); and also of the unreasonableness of the conduct of the payee subsequent to the payment - for example, where he suffers heavy losses as a result of making highly speculative investments. Another important issue is whether the defence should be available where the loss is due not to the payee's reliance but to some other factor, such as where the money mistakenly paid is stolen from the payee. In this case the enrichment is illusory and we think it would be unjust to order repayment.[126]

2.73   Finally, there is the relationship between the defence of change of position and the existing defence of estoppel. Given that the House of Lords has now held that English law recognises that a claim to restitution based on unjust enrichment may be met by the defence that the defendant has changed his position in good faith, should the estoppel defence be retained at all, and, if so, in what circumstances should it apply?[127]

2.74   Both the New Zealand and Western Australian legislation consist of a general formula which leaves most of these questions to the courts. The New Zealand provision[128] provides that:

> "Relief, whether under section ninety-four A of this Act or in equity or otherwise, in respect of any payment made under mistake, whether of law or of fact, shall be denied wholly or in part if the person from whom relief is sought received the payment in good faith and has so altered his position in reliance on the validity of the payment that in the opinion of the Court, having regard to all possible implications in respect of other persons, it is inequitable to grant relief, or to grant relief in full, as the case may be."

---

126.   See Lipkin Gorman v. Karpnale Ltd., [1991] 3 W.L.R. 10, 16 per Lord Templeman (a plaintiff must show that the defendant was unjustly enriched and remained unjustly enriched). See also Goff & Jones, pp. 693-4; Needham, op cit. Cf. the position of money lent which is stolen from the debtor, which still has to be repaid. But there the basis of liability is agreement not enrichment.

127.   See Birks, "The Recovery of Carelessly Mistaken Payments", [1972] C.L.P. 179.

128.   Section 94B of the Judicature Amendment Act 1958.

This provision applies only where relief is sought on the ground of mistake. It is also limited to the case where there has been reliance on the payment by the payee. It does not therefore apply where the payment has been stolen after receipt. Apart from this, the requirement that relief be refused where it is inequitable to grant it, leaves the courts with considerable flexibility.

2.75   The Western Australian legislation[129] is identical to the New Zealand legislation, except that it specifically directs the court to disregard the position of the payer in deciding whether it is equitable to grant relief. The Law Reform Committee of South Australia[130] has also recommended that the New Zealand model be followed subject to a specific requirement that any alteration of position should reasonably flow from the mistake.

2.76   It has been suggested that a disadvantage of this approach is that it produces a position which is too vague to be satisfactory in commercial contexts.[131] However, some degree of uncertainty is inevitable whenever a new doctrine is introduced whilst its precise scope and operation is determined by the courts. A statutory formula

---

129.   Section 24 of the Law Reform (Property Perpetuities, and Succession) Act 1962, subsequently repealed and re-enacted as section 125 of the Property Law Act, 1969 (WA).

130.   Report relating to the Irrecoverability of Benefits Obtained by Reason of Mistake of Law, (84th Report, 1984) pp. 31-32.

131.   Sutton, "Mistake of Law-Lifting the Lid of Pandora's Box" in The A.G. Davis Essays in Law (ed Northey) Ch.9, p.238.

of this kind appears no vaguer than the judicial formulations in other jurisdictions, and it may be seen as the role of the courts to introduce certainty into the law through the development of detailed rules to govern the operation of the defence.

2.77   However, there may be some force in a contention that statutory, as opposed to judicial, promulgation of such a generally worded formula, may be both more productive of uncertainty and more likely to lead to undesirable results. This is because the courts may in some circumstances interpret a flexible statutory provision as permitting a discretionary power of adjustment rather than one based on principle.   The New Zealand Court of Appeal in Thomas v. Houston Corbett[132] interpreted the New Zealand provision as giving them a power to split the loss between the two parties, rather than simply refusing recovery to the extent of the payee's reliance.   It has been argued[133] that this was never intended and is out of line with the common law approach.

2.78   Our provisional view is that there should not be statutory refinement of the defence of change of position. The breadth of the statutory formulations in other jurisdictions does not offer advantages in terms of certainty compared with the broad defence recognised by the House of Lords.   Moreover, a statutory formulation may have the effect of freezing further common law development.[134] However, we seek the views of consultees on this question.

---

132.   [1969] N.Z.L.R. 151.

133.   See the British Columbia Law Reform Commission, LRC 51 (1981) p. 79.   See also the South Australian Law Reform Committee (84th Report, 1984), p. 32.

134.   See Murphy v. Brentwood D.C. [1990] 3 W.L.R. 414, 419, 433, 441, 451, 457.

In particular we seek views as to the scope and operation of the defence:

(a) the type of reliance which constitutes a change of position,

(b) the relevance of fault and,

(c) the relationship of the defence of change of position with the defence of estoppel.

2.79   Finally, there are a number of existing statutory provisions giving restitutionary rights.[135]   These concern overpayments made to and by public authorities and will be examined in the next two parts of this paper together with the applicability of the defence of change of position to public authorities.[136]

---

135.   See paras. 3.20-3.37 and 4.5. below.

136.   See paras. 3.77-3.78 below.

PART III: CLAIMS IN RESPECT OF ULTRA VIRES PAYMENTS MADE TO PUBLIC BODIES

3.1   In a number of cases the question has arisen as to whether a citizen may recover a payment which he has made in response to a demand by the government or a public authority which there is no power to make. The demand may be for the payment of tax or for payment of a fee for the provision of goods or services. It may be invalid because the government misconstrued the provision providing for a particular type of payment; because the provision relied on is itself invalid, for example where the charge is imposed by delegated legislation which is outside the terms of the enabling statute; or because there is no provision for such a charge at all. A demand may be invalid because it infringes the principles of domestic administrative law, or of European Community law. A like problem arises where the payment is made before there has been a demand but in respect of a charge which there is no power to levy.

1.   THE CURRENT LAW

(a) Recovery under the Common Law

(i)   The General Principle

3.2   Although, as will be seen, the common law has been substantially modified by statute, the general principle upon which it is based remains of importance. There are two approaches. The first, generally accepted to be the law prior to the decision of the Court of Appeal in Woolwich

Equitable Building Society v. I.R.C.,[1] is that any ultra
vires payments are recoverable on the same basis as any
other payments made to another which are not lawfully due.
The payer will be able to recover if he can show that one of
the ordinary grounds for restitution exists. Thus he will
be able to recover if he can show, for example, that the
payment was made as a result of a mistake of fact;[2] or under
duress;[3] or pursuant to an agreement that the sum would be
repaid if it were found not in fact to be due.[4] Conversely
there is no special rule of recovery which applies to these
situations: subject to limited exceptions, which will be
discussed below,[5] the citizen cannot generally recover the
payment simply because of its ultra vires nature.

3.3   The second approach, now enshrined in the majority
decision in Woolwich Equitable Building Society v. I.R.C.,
distinguishes public and private law and recognises a
general right to restitution in cases of payments in
response to ultra vires demands by government or public
authorities. The Woolwich case concerned the return of
payments made by the building society in respect of deposits

---

1. The Times, 27 May 1991 (Glidewell and Butler-Sloss
   L.JJ., Ralph Gibson L.J. dissenting), reversing Nolan J,
   [1989] 1 W.L.R. 137. In associated proceedings the
   House of Lords held that the demand was ultra vires: R.
   v. I.R.C., Ex p. Woolwich Equitable Building Society
   [1990] 1 W.L.R. 1400

2. Meadows v. Grand Junction Waterworks Co. (1905) 21
   T.L.R. 538.

3. Maskell v. Horner [1915] 3 K.B. 106; Mason v. New South
   Wales (1959) 102 C.L.R. 108 (H.C. Aust.)

4. Sebel Products Ltd. v. Commissioners of Customs and
   Excise [1949] Ch. 409; Woolwich Equitable Building
   Society v. I.R.C., [1989] 1 W.L.R. 137 (Nolan J.); The
   Times, 27 May 1991 (C.A.).

5. See para. 3.9-3.12 below.

with it which were held not to be due as the regulations pursuant to which the payments were made were found to be ultra vires.[6] The general right to restitution set out in Woolwich is, however, subject to a number of limitations, including one based on the mistake of law rule. Under both approaches, therefore, a payment made under mistake of law is irrecoverable in the absence of another ground for restitution. Although the general public law restitutionary principle is now the law, both approaches will be set out below. First, an account of the traditional approach will assist in the analysis of the principle enunciated in the Woolwich case. Secondly, we understand that there is to be an appeal to the House of Lords and the traditional approach cannot be finally discarded before the outcome of that appeal.

(ii)   The Traditional Formulation

3.4   The applicability of the ordinary private law was established in a series of first instance cases. In Slater v. Burnley Corporation[7] the corporation had demanded from the plaintiff a higher water rate than the relevant statute required him to pay. He had objected but paid. It was argued that recovery should be allowed simply because of the unlawful nature of the demand; but it was held that there could be no recovery in the absence of a distinct ground for restitution, such as duress. In William Whiteley Ltd v. R.[8] the plaintiff sought to recover payments for licences claimed by the Revenue in respect of certain canteen workers

---

6. R. v. I.R.C., Ex p. Woolwich Equitable Building Society [1990] 1 W.L.R. 1400.

7. (1888) 59 L.T. 636.

8. (1909) 101 L.T. 741.

employed by the plaintiff, on the basis that they were "male servants" under the legislation. The plaintiff disputed this interpretation and contended that no licences were needed but nevertheless paid the charges. Eventually he successfully disputed the Revenue's interpretation in the courts and sought to recover the overpayments. Walton J. rejected the contention that money unlawfully demanded by a public official may automatically be recovered; and held that there could be no recovery since none of the ordinary grounds for recovery had been made out.[9] This approach was confirmed by the Court of Appeal in National Pari-Mutuel Association Ltd v. R.[10] in the context of a payment made as a result of a mistaken construction of a statute. The Association had paid duty to the Revenue in respect of a private totaliser. When it became apparent that there was no liability to pay they sought to recover the sums paid but were unsuccessful: the payments had been made under a mistake of law, which is not a ground for recovery. Although subject to much criticism,[11] this approach was confirmed recently by the Court of Appeal in R. v. Richmond upon Thames L.B.C., Ex parte Stubbs.[12] The same approach

---

9. See also Twyford v. Manchester Corporation [1946] Ch. 236.

10. (1930) 47 T.L.R. 110.

11. For the argument that, despite the above cases, the weight of the authorities supports a right to recovery, see Birks, pp. 294-299; "Restitution from Public Authorities" [1980] C.L.P. 191; "Restitution from the Executive: a Tercentenary Footnote to the Bill of Rights" in Essays on Restitution (ed. Finn, 1990), pp. 177-183 relying primarily on (a) cases concerned with the performance of a public duty, discussed below at para. 3.10 and (b) Hooper v. Exeter Corporation (1887) 56 L.J.Q.B. 457.

12. (1989) 87 L.G.R. 637. And see also Woodcock v. Commissioners of Customs and Excise [1989] S.T.C. 237.

has also been followed in Scotland,[13] in certain Commonwealth jurisdictions,[14] and by Nolan J at first instance and in the dissenting judgment of Ralph Gibson L.J. in the Woolwich case.[15]

3.5   The application of the mistake of fact ground to public authorities requires little discussion, since it does not appear to have created any difficulty in the English case law. Recovery on the basis of duress has been a little more problematic. It is clear that a threat to the person or property of the plaintiff if the invalid demand is not met is an illegitimate threat for the purposes of the law of duress. Thus, a person who pays in order to avoid the threatened action may recover on the ground of duress.[16] A threat to act in an ultra vires manner - for example, by withholding a benefit which there is a duty to provide - is also treated as illegitimate.[17] On the other hand a mere threat to sue if payment is not made is not sufficient to constitute such a threat as was illustrated by both William

---

13. Glasgow Corporation v. Lord Advocate 1959 S.C. 203.

14. Mason v. New South Wales (1959) 102 C.L.R. 108 (Australia); Eadie v. Township of Brantford [1967] S.C.R. 573 (Canada). Following the decision by the Supreme Court of Canada in Air Canada v. British Columbia [1989] 1 S.C.R. 1161 recovery will now be allowed when the payment is made under a mistake of law although not where the relevant provision is unconstitutional but, where no mistake has been made, the mere fact that a levied payment is ultra vires is still not in itself a ground for recovery.

15. [1989] 1 W.L.R. 137.

16. E.g. Mason v. New South Wales (1959) 102 C.L.R. 108.

17. The cases concerned with payments for the performance of a public duty, discussed below, could be explained on this basis: see para. 3.10 below.

Whiteley Ltd. v. R. and Woolwich Equitable Building Society
v. I.R.C..

3.6   These principles are clear enough but it may be
difficult to decide whether there is duress where the
authority does not explicitly make a threat. Often
sanctions which the plaintiff may expect to be applied if no
payment is made may be provided in the statute for
non-payment, for example a licence may be refused or goods
seized. The mere existence of these sanctions is not
necessarily sufficient to establish a threat but the courts
have differed in their willingness to imply a threat in such
circumstances.

3.7   In Twyford v. Manchester Corporation,[18] stonemasons
sought to recover a fee which had been unlawfully demanded
from them for admission to a cemetery to carry out their
work but it was held there had been no implied threat to
exclude them for non-payment. Again, in Woolwich Equitable
Building Society v. I.R.C., there was no evidence of conduct
by the Revenue amounting to duress. Specifically, the fact
that interest would be payable on any sum withheld if the
challenge to the regulations failed, which could not be
deducted from future profits, did not constitute duress.
Neither did the fact that the building society could have
anticipated the raising of an assessment or the issue of a
writ, both involving highly undesirable and commercially
unacceptable adverse publicity.[19] On the other hand,

---

18. [1946] Ch. 236. For criticism see Marsh, (1946) 62
L.Q.R. 333, Birks, pp. 294-9; "Restitution from Public
Authorities" [1980] C.L.P. 191; Goff and Jones, pp.
242-3.

19. [1989] 1 W.L.R. 137, 143, 146; The Times, 27 May 1991
(C.A.).

in <u>Mason</u> v. <u>New South Wales</u>[20] the High Court of Australia was prepared to find duress when the plaintiffs paid a fee for a licence to carry goods, under a scheme which was later held to be unconstitutional. The duress was said to lie in the fact that the state <u>might</u> have seized the plaintiffs' vehicles had they operated without a licence (a power which they appeared to have under the legislation), although it seemed that such seizure had in fact been rare in the past and certainly had not been explicitly threatened. Although "the ability of the Crown or a public authority to apply duress to the subject may be very much greater than that of another subject",[21] the availability of the duress ground to recover an unlawful levy depends on the court's interpretation of the facts.

3.8   So far as the question of a contract to repay is concerned, it is possible that the courts may be more willing to imply such a contract where the defendant is a public authority than in other cases. In <u>Woolwich Equitable Building Society</u> v. <u>I.R.C.</u> Nolan J stated that "whenever money is paid to the revenue pending the outcome of a dispute which, to the knowledge of both parties, will determine whether or not the revenue are entitled to the money, an agreement for the repayment of the money if and when the dispute is resolved in the taxpayer's favour must inevitably be implied unless the statute itself produces that result".[22]

---

20. (1959) 102 C.L.R. 108.

21. <u>Woolwich Equitable Building Society</u> v. <u>I.R.C.</u> [1989] 1 W.L.R. 137, 144 (Nolan J).

22. Ibid., 147, following <u>Sebel Products Ltd.</u> v. <u>Commissioners of Customs and Excise</u> [1949] Ch. 409. See also The Times, 27 May 1991 (C.A.).

Exceptions to the Traditional Formulation of the General Principle

3.9   There are suggestions in the case law that there are certain common law exceptions to the general principle, although few appear to be clearly established.

Payments Demanded for the Performance of a Public Duty

3.10   A number of cases can be read as supporting a proposition that all payments unlawfully demanded for the performance of a public duty are recoverable. Some have treated these cases as merely an example of the ordinary law of duress, in which the courts have been willing to find an implied threat to withhold performance for non payment.[23] Others have suggested, however, that these cases are really based on a more general principle which allows recovery in such circumstances regardless of the existence of duress, since they do not address the question of whether there was actually any threat made by the authority[24] and these cases form the basis of the Court of Appeal's enunciation of a general principle of restitution in public law in the Woolwich case. Although most predate the decisions supporting the traditional approach applying the ordinary private law, in South of Scotland Electricity Board v. British Oxygen Co. Ltd. (No. 2) the House of Lords, albeit without directing recovery since the facts had not been

---

23. e.g. Craig, Administrative Law (2nd ed., 1989), p.468; Goff and Jones, pp.216-222.

24. Birks, [1980] C.L.P. 191; Essays on Restitution (ed. Finn, 1990), pp. 177-178 argues, on the basis of Hooper v. Exeter Corporation (1887) 56 L.J.Q.B. 457, that the exception extends to all cases where there is an unlawful demand and the authority is in a position to dictate terms in other ways than by withholding what it is its business to provide.

found, thought that once it had been established that the Board's charges contravened statutory restrictions there would be no problem in the company recovering them.[25] It has been argued that Steele v. Williams[26] provides stronger support. In that case a fee was demanded from the plaintiff for extracts taken from a parish register. In fact no such fee was due, and the plaintiff, who had paid, was allowed to recover it. It has been argued that the fee was actually claimed after the plaintiff had obtained the extracts. If so the only basis of recovery would appear to be the fact of the invalid payment made for the performance of the duty.[27] Other cases which have been relied on for a wider principle include Campbell v. Hall,[28] Dew v. Parsons,[29] and Hooper v. Exeter Corporation.[30] It is, however, difficult to reconcile these cases with more recent decisions, in particular Twyford or the reasoning in Slater v. Burnley Corporation and William Whiteley Ltd v. R., and, until the Court of Appeal decision in the Woolwich case, the more recent decisions were taken to preclude a wider principle.

---

25. [1959] 1 W.L.R. 587. But note this case (a) did not consider Glasgow Corporation v. Lord Advocate 1959 S.C. 203 or William Whiteley Ltd v. R. (1909) 101 L.T. 741 which adopted the traditional approach, (b) was concerned with the construction of the particular legislation and cases decided upon the railway legislation and, (c) was regarded by two of their Lordships (Viscount Kilmuir L.C. and Lord Merriman) as in effect a duress case since electricity users had no choice but to pay if they were to receive electricity.

26. (1853) 22 L.J. Ex. 225.

27. Birks, p. 297; "Restitution from the Executive: a Tercentenary Footnote to the Bill of Rights" in Essays on Restitution (ed. Finn, 1990), pp. 178-179; Cf. "Restitution from Public Authorities" [1980] C.L.P. 191, 201. But see the statement of facts in 17 Jur. 464 and the judgment of Parke B. who clearly treats the case as one of duress.

28. (1774) 1 Cowp. 204.

"Recovery" through a Set-Off against Money Owed

3.11   In Blackpool and Fleetwood Tramroad Co. v. Bispham with Norbreck U.D.C.,[31] it was stated that sums paid to a public authority pursuant to an unlawful rating demand, although they might be irrecoverable if an action were brought for repayment, could be set off against sums owed by the payer to the same authority. This alleged rule was referred to by Lord Bridge in the House of Lords in R. v. Tower Hamlets L.B.C., Ex parte Chetnik Developments Ltd[32] who commented that it "seems to produce an anomaly" in allowing a set-off but not a direct action for recovery. His Lordship did not expressly state whether he regarded the decision as correct nor what was the scope of any principle which it might be considered to lay down, for example whether it applied in contexts other than rating. The tenor of his speech, including the reference to the anomaly, suggests that he doubted the correctness of the Blackpool decision.[33]

Payments made to an Officer of Court

3.12   It was explained in Part II[34] that the mistake of

---

29. (1819) 2 B & Ald. 562.

30. (1887) 57 L.J.Q.B. 457.

31. [1910] 1 K.B. 592.

32. [1988] A.C. 858.

33. It may be noted, however, that a similar "anomaly" exists in relation to overpayments by trustees and personal representatives (para. 2.13 above) and another has been created by legislation in relation to overpayment of certain welfare benefits: see para. 4.5 below.

34. Para. 2.14 above.

law rule does not apply where a payment is made to an officer of the court. The exception does not concern invalid levies, but in principle it should cover the case of an officer of the court who demands a payment which is outside his statutory authority.

(iii)   A General Restitutionary Principle

3.13   In Woolwich Equitable Building Society v. I.R.C. the Court of Appeal held that a person who makes a payment in response to an unlawful demand for tax, or any like demand from a public official, i.e. a demand for which there is no basis in law, immediately acquires a prima facie right to be repaid the amount as money had and received. It was stated that the general principle is subject to two limitations. It does not apply where a payment is made in circumstances implying that it is paid voluntarily to close the transaction, a term we understand to include payments in submission to or compromise of the claim. Secondly, although the scope of this limitation is not entirely clear, the general principle does not apply where the payment is made under mistake of law. Such payments will not be recoverable. The uncertainty in the second limitation stems from the different way it was formulated. Gildewell L.J.'s formulation only excluded payments under a mistake as to the proper interpretation of a statute (but possibly not of an ultra vires regulation) but Butler-Sloss L.J. stated that (subject to the reviewability of a decision to refuse repayment)[35] all payments made under mistake of law fell outside the general principle.[36] The general

---

[35.] On which see R. v. Tower Hamlets L.B.C., Ex p. Chetnik Developments Ltd. [1988] A.C. 858, paras. 3.16-3.18 below.

[36.] As Ralph Gibson L.J., dissenting, stated that "the mistake of law rule is a central part of the law of

restitutionary principle may also be subject to a third
limitation, requiring the invalidity of the demand to have
been established in judicial review proceedings, although no
concluded view was expressed. None of these limitations
applied on the facts of the Woolwich case; judicial review
proceedings had succeeded,[37] the building society had always
challenged the validity of the regulations and it was not
under any kind of mistake.

3.14 The restitutionary principle was based upon "a
general standard of fairness in the relations and dealings
between officers and organs of Government who require the
payment of a tax or customs duty, and the taxpayer"[38] who is
likely to be at a disadvantage. It was distilled from a
number of sources:-

(a) the prohibition in Article 4 of the Bill of Rights
    on "levying money for or to the use of the Crowne
    by [pretence] of prerogative without grant of
    Parlyament...",[39]

(b) public duty cases which could not be explained as
    "withholding" or duress cases[40] and,

---

36. Continued
    restitution", there appears to be a majority for the
    irrecoverability of all payments under mistake of law.

37. R. v. I.R.C., Ex p. Woolwich Equitable Building Society
    [1990] 1 W.L.R. 1400.

38. Per Glidewell L.J.

39. (1688) 1 Will. & Mar., sess 2, c 2, on which see
    Attorney-General v. Wilts United Dairies Ltd. (1921) 37
    T.L.R., 884, 886 (Atkin L.J.).

40. See para. 3.10 above.

(c)   the general approach of the House of Lords in R. v.
      Tower Hamlets L.B.C., Ex parte Chetnik Developments
      Ltd.,[41] to the review of a decision not to refund
      overpaid rates.

Glidewell L.J. said the cases supporting the traditional
approach were either distinguishable, as examples of
payments to close the transaction[42] or made under mistake of
law,[43] or wrong.   Butler-Sloss L.J. was inclined to think
that although they had stood for many years, these cases
were wrongly decided.

3.15   Ralph Gibson L.J.'s dissent, in which he favoured
the traditional approach was influenced by three
considerations. First, the mistake of law limitation to the
general restitutionary principle was unsatisfactory and
suggested that no such general right existed. A right of
recovery based on general considerations of justice should
be equally available to a payer under a mistake of law and
there was no relevant distinction between a demand based on
the honest but mistaken construction of a valid provision
and one based on a bona fide belief that an invalid
provision had been lawfully enacted. Secondly, while the
law could have developed a general rule of recovery, the
cases on which the traditional approach was based did not do

---

41. [1988] A.C. 858, considered at para. 3.17 below.

42. Slater v. Burnley Corporation (1888) 59 L.T. 636;
     William Whiteley Ltd. v. R. (1909) 101 L.T. 741, para.
     3.4 above; Twyford v. Manchester Corporation [1946] Ch.
     236, para. 3.7 above.

43. National Pari-Mutuel Association Ltd. v. R. (1930) 47
     T.L.R. 110, para 3.4 above; Glasgow Corporation v. Lord
     Advocate 1959 S.C. 203. Although Walton J., in William
     Whiteley Ltd. v. R. (1909) 101 L.T. 741, based his
     decision in part on mistake of law, on the facts this
     was said by Glidewell J. not to be justified.

this. He attributes this to the wider public interest in security of receipts and a concern that the wholesale opening up of transactions would impose grave difficulties for tax authorities and introduce unwarrantable uncertainty into relations between the taxpayer and the Exchequer.[44] Thirdly, the traditional approach has stood without effective challenge for many years and legislation, which apparently assumes that it is correct and that there is no general right of recovery in public law cases, had been passed.[45]

(iv)   Application for Judicial Review

3.16   Where there is no right in restitution to the recovery of an invalidly demanded payment, there may be a discretion to make a repayment and indeed such discretion has been exercised in practice: for example, prior to the introduction of a legislative right to recover, we understand that it was the practice to repay excess payments of V.A.T. though made under an error of law, unless the payee would have gained a windfall because he had passed on all or part of the tax to his customers. In some cases there may be an express statutory discretion;[46] in others the authority's right to repay will depend on the general law concerning the making of ex gratia payments.[47] Where

---

[44.] Reliance was placed on Glasgow Corporation v. Lord Advocate 1959 S.C. 203, 230. See also para. 2.34 above.

[45.] Reference was made to Taxes Management Act 1970, section 33 and General Rate Act 1967, section 9. For these and other statutory provisions, see paras. 3.20-3.37 below.

[46.] See Customs and Excise Management Act 1979, section 127.

[47.] The Crown has a general power under the common law to make ex gratia payments. Doubts were expressed by the Joint Committee on Statutory Instruments (1988/1989 H.C. 47-i pp.7 & 23) as to whether a power to make provision in subordinate legislation for payment

there is discretion, whether conferred specifically by statute or not, it is reviewable according to the usual principles of judicial review. Thus, in exercising it, the authority must take into account only relevant considerations, and must not act for improper purposes or in bad faith.

3.17   In R. v. Tower Hamlets L.B.C., Ex parte Chetnik Developments Ltd.[48] the House of Lords considered a local authority's exercise of a statutory discretion to refund an overpayment. Judicial review was sought of the authority's refusal to return an overpayment of rates, a decision made in the exercise of an express statutory discretion to refund in the General Rate Act 1967.[49] The action succeeded and Lord Bridge stated that, under the statute, the fact that the payment was made under a mistake of law was not a consideration which would justify refusing recovery.[50] Nor could recovery be refused because of the special financial difficulties which would otherwise be faced by the authority. He seemed to envisage that recovery could be refused only in those types of case where recovery would be denied in a common law action based on mistake of fact, such as where there was a compromise of a disputed claim, although this general principle was not specifically stated by his Lordship. Lord Goff, however, did go so far as to

---

47. Continued
     of fees and charges could also be construed as conferring a power to make regulations giving a right to recover. Section 128 of the Finance Act 1990 validates such a practice only in respect of enactments preceding it. See paras. 3.36-3.37 below.

48. [1988] A.C. 858.

49. Section 9 (1)(e).

50. [1988] A.C. 858, 877.

say that the section effectively created a "statutory remedy of restitution"[51] to prevent the authority's unjust enrichment at the expense of the ratepayer, and the courts should have regard to general restitutionary principles (including change of position) in deciding whether the authority could lawfully refuse recovery.

3.18   If, as was considered the position in the Woolwich case, these principles apply to the review of any discretion to repay, whether or not deriving from a specific statutory provision, there would be an effective ability to recover in any case where a discretion to repay exists.   Even if the traditional approach is reinstated by the House of Lords, a substantial inroad would be made into the operation of private law in this area, albeit one based on judicial review, a discretionary process, rather than rights. However, the speeches in Chetnik appear to be based very specifically on the intention of Parliament in conferring the particular power to refund which was in issue in that case.   Thus, for example, Lord Goff stated that it was the section which creates the right to recover and Lord Bridge referred specifically to the intentions of Parliament in enacting the provision.   It should also be noted that, although this particular action was brought by way of judicial review, the Act did provide a right of appeal to the courts,[52] thus specifically indicating that in this context the courts were to have the final word on the merits.   Where the courts' role is exclusively supervisory and there is no express discretion to repay, they may be more cautious in using judicial review.

---

51. Ibid, 882.

52. The question of whether review ought to have been refused because of the alternative remedy by way of appeal was not taken.

(v) Summary

3.19   At common law the position of payments made by way
of taxes or charges which turn out not to be lawfully due is
as follows.   They will generally be irrecoverable on either
of the two approaches considered if made under a mistake of
law, that is if paid in the belief that there is or may be
liability to pay when in fact there is no such liability
under the relevant provision properly construed.   In other
cases payment may be made in circumstances where liability
is denied.   Here there is a difference between the two
approaches.   The traditional approach only allowed recovery
where duress could be shown or where there was an implied
agreement to repay the sum.   The effect of the Court of
Appeal's decision in Woolwich Equitable Building Society v.
I.R.C. is to allow recovery in all cases where payment was
not made to close the transaction.   These principles may
require some qualification because of the exceptions
mentioned above and the operation of the principles of
judicial review, but the extent of such qualification is
somewhat uncertain.

(b)   Statutory Provisions for Recovery

3.20   In certain contexts the common law has been
abrogated or modified by statutory rights to recover
payments made to public authorities.   In the Woolwich case
although, as we have seen, one of the factors leading Ralph
Gibson L.J. to reject the general restitutionary principle
was the existence of legislation which appears to assume
that there is no general right of recovery, the majority's
treatment of statutory rights of recovery was brief.   In
this section the most important of the statutory provisions
will be set out and their treatment in the Woolwich case
will then be considered.

74

3.21   Section 24 of the Finance Act 1989[53] provides that "[w]here a person has paid an amount to the [Customs and Excise] Commissioners by way of value added tax which was not tax due to them, they shall be liable to repay the amount to him"[54] on a claim being made for the purpose.[55] This provision gives a general right to recover a tax not due which does not depend on the circumstances of payment: it is irrelevant, for example, whether the payment was made under a mistake.   The limitation period is six years from the date on which the payment was made; but where the payment is made by reason of mistake a claim may be brought at any time within the expiry of six years from the time the claimant discovered the mistake, or could with reasonable diligence have discovered it.[56]   There appears to be no legal right to interest on the amount repaid.[57]

3.22   It is a defence to any claim under the section that repayment "would unjustly enrich" the claimant.[58]   This

---

53. The section was brought into force by S.I. 1989, No. 2271.

54. Section 24(1). The procedures are set out in S.I. 1989, No. 2248, Reg. 6.

55. Section 24(2).

56. Section 24(5).

57. With respect to a claim adjudicated by a V.A.T. tribunal, as is the case with relief under section 24, a specific provision is required to enable interest to be ordered to be paid to the applicant. No such provision applies to claims under section 24. See, however, Finance Bill 1991, clause 16, making provision for interest where there has been error on the part of the Commissioners.

58. Section 24(3).

provision is designed to preclude recovery when the payee has passed on the amount of the tax, for example to purchasers of his goods or services. It is possible that it could be used also in other circumstances; for example to prevent recovery where the payment was made in respect of a statute barred debt.

3.23   The section specifically states that there is to be no liability to repay by virtue of the fact that it was not tax due except under the section.[59]

(ii)   Excise Duty and Car Tax

3.24   Section 29 of the Finance Act 1989 governs the recovery of overpaid excise duty and car tax. It provides that proceedings for restitution of such amounts "shall not be dismissed by reason only of the fact that the amount was paid by reason of a mistake of law".[60] This provision has already been discussed in paragraphs 2.53-54 above. It was explained that the intention appears to be that such payments made under a mistake of law should be recoverable on the same basis as payments made under a mistake of fact. In contrast with section 24 concerning V.A.T., section 29 only applies to mistaken payments and does not apply to all cases where the payment is not lawfully due. Insofar as the section succeeds in assimilating the position with mistake of law to that which applies to mistake of fact, the common law rules on defences, limitation periods etc which apply to mistake of fact will apply. In the case of car tax it

---

[59.] Section 24(7).

[60.] Section 29(2).

appears that interest should be payable on any sum repaid[61] but it is not so clear whether it would be legally payable in respect of overpaid excise duty.[62] The section specifically provides that the defence of "unjust enrichment" shall be available[63] as it is under section 24.

(iii)   Income Tax, Corporation Tax, Capital Gains Tax and Petroleum Revenue Tax[64]

3.25   Section 33 of the Taxes Management Act 1970 makes provision for the recovery of overpaid Income Tax, Corporation Tax, Capital Gains Tax and Petroleum Revenue Tax where there is an excessive assessment by reason of "error or mistake" in any tax return. Thus, it is not a general right to recover tax not due, as in section 24 of the Finance Act 1989, but depends on proof of "error or mistake". It applies to errors and mistakes both of fact and law[65] but is limited in that no relief is to be given "in respect of an error or mistake as to the basis on which

---

[61]. Since any action for recovery is, by contrast with an action under section 24, brought by writ, interest should be available under Supreme Court Act 1981, section 35A.

[62]. The action will be brought by writ, so that section 35A applies. However, under the Customs and Excise Management Act, 1979 section 116A, an amount of excise duty is deemed due on an estimation until properly challenged. The obligation to refund therefore does not arise until the challenge is made and interest may only be payable from that date.

[63]. Section 29(3).

[64]. The relevant provisions are discussed in Stopforth, "Error or Mistake Relief" (1989) 5 B.T.R. 151; Simon's Taxes, Division A 3.10.

[65]. Heastie v. Veitch & Co (1933) 18 T.C. 305 (error of mixed fact and law); Barlow v. I.R.C. (1937) 21 T.C. 354 (error of law).

the liability ... ought to have been computed where the return was in fact made on the basis or in accordance with the practice generally prevailing at the time when the return was made."[66] This important limitation is designed to preclude recovery where many persons are affected by the same error and a right to recover might thus disrupt the conduct of Revenue business or even of government finances. Applications for relief are made to the Board of Inland Revenue which is required to give such relief as is "reasonable and just."[67] The question of what relief is "reasonable and just" is a matter for the Board itself to decide subject to appeal to the Special Commissioners. There is no general right to require a case to be stated on a point of law where relief is sought under the section, which includes the question of what constitutes reasonable and just relief;[68] although it is possible that a court could determine this question on an application for judicial review for error of law.[69] So far as can be ascertained, it appears that relief is normally given; the section is

---

66. Proviso to section 33(2). This restriction is long standing; see Finance Act 1923, section 24. See generally para. 3.74 below.

67. Section 33(2). The Board is directed by section 33(3) to "have regard to all the relevant circumstances ...and in particular...whether the granting of relief would result in the exclusion from charge to tax of any part of the profits of the claimant, and for this purpose the Board may take into consideration the liability of the claimant and assessments made on him in respect of chargeable periods other than that to which the claim relates." This is designed to ensure that the taxpayer does not gain a windfall benefit from recovery.

68. See section 33(4). The case stated procedure is limited to a point of law arising in connection with the computation of profits.

69. The availability of judicial review for error of law is a question which is complex and uncertain: see, for example, H.W.R. Wade, Administrative Law (6th ed., 1988), p. 299 et seq.

regarded as affording a prima facie right to relief where it applies.

3.26   A "repayment supplement" may be available where repayment is made more than a certain time after the original payment.[70]

(iv)   Inheritance Tax

3.27   Limited provision is made for the recovery of overpaid Inheritance Tax in section 241 of the Inheritance Tax Act 1984.[71] Section 241(1) provides that where it has been proved to the Board that too much tax has been paid the Board is required to repay the excess.   This right of recovery is not dependent on proof of any error by the payer.   The provision is however, limited in a similar way to section 33 of the Taxes Management Act 1970: section 255 of the Inheritance Tax Act provides effectively that there shall be no recovery where the payment is made and accepted "on a view of the law then generally received or adopted in practice."[72]

---

70. Income and Corporation Taxes Act 1988, sections 824 and 825; section 47 of the Finance (No.2) Act 1975 (capital gains tax), on which see R. v. Inland Revenue Commissioners, Ex p. Commerzbank AG, [1991] S.T.C. 271. But where the payment of tax has not been postponed pending an appeal, there is no provision for the payment of interest in respect of any overpayment; Taxes Management Act 1970, section 55.

71. The provisions (originally in Finance Act 1894, section 8(12), qualified by Finance Act 1951, section 35 relating to estate duty) are discussed in Dymond's Capital Taxes, paras. 28.1210-28.1227.

72. Inheritance Tax Act 1984, section 255.   See para. 3.74 below.

3.28   Interest is payable on the amount returned.[73]

3.29   There is no obligation to repay where the claim for repayment is made more than six years after the payment of the tax in respect of which recovery is sought.[74]

(v)   Stamp Duty[75]

3.30   Section 13(4) of the Stamp Act 1891 confers a right to the recovery of Stamp Duty which has been paid in conformity with an erroneous assessment. The right does not depend on any error by the payer. The court is empowered to award interest on the amount recovered.[76]

(vi)   Social Security Contributions

3.31   There is a provision in the Social Security (Contributions) Regulations 1979[77] which gives a right to the recovery of National Insurance Contributions paid in error.[78] This provision applies whether the mistake is one

---

[73.]   Inheritance Tax Act 1984, section 235.

[74.]   Inheritance Tax Act 1984, section 241.

[75.]   The provisions are discussed in Sergeant and Sims on Stamp Duties (9th ed., 1988), pp. 77-79.

[76.]   Finance Act 1965, section 91.

[77.]   S.I. 1979 No. 591 as amended, see Halsbury's Statutory Instruments, Vol. 18, pp. 75-76.

[78.]   Ibid, Reg. 32; and see also Reg. 34 on voluntary contributions where recovery is not stated to depend on the existence of any error.

of fact or law.[79]

(vii)   Community Charge and Non-Domestic Rates

3.32   With respect to the Community Charge and
non-domestic rates general provision has been made in
regulations for the recovery of overpayments.[80]   These
provisions apply where there has been an overpayment
following an excess demand in a notice issued by the
charging authority, and thus do not depend on proof of a
mistake by the payer. Provision is made for the payment of
interest in certain cases in which, in consequence of an
alteration to a valuation list compiled under Part III of
the Local Government Finance Act 1988 (non-domestic rating),
an amount falls to be repaid or credited by a charging
authority or the Secretary of State.[81]

---

[79]. Morecombe v. Secretary of State, The Times, December 12
1987.

[80]. The principal examples are S.I. 1989 No. 438 Reg. 26
(The Community Charges (Administration and Enforcement)
Regulations 1989);   S.I. 1989 No. 1058 Reg. 9 (The
Non-Domestic Rating ((Collection and Enforcement)
(Local Lists)) Regulations 1989);   S.I. 1989 No. 2260
Reg. 9 (The Non-Domestic Rating (Collection and
Enforcement) (Central Lists)) Regulations 1989).   For
the position under the old rating system, see section 9
of the General Rate Act 1967.   At the present time the
details of the council tax which will replace the
community charge are unknown.

[81]. S.I. 1990 No. 1904 (The Non-Domestic Rating (Payment of
Interest) Regulations).

(viii) Import Duties

3.33   The recovery of import duties not lawfully payable
is governed by section 127 of the Customs and Excise
Management Act 1979.   The dispute must arise before the
delivery of the goods and section 127 simply provides for a
method of challenge, as an alternative to that of
withholding payment, which is not permitted.   The importer
must pay the amount demanded, but may then require the
matter to be referred to the High Court or, where the issue
concerns the valuation of goods, to a referee.   If on such a
reference it is determined that there has been an
overpayment, the amount overpaid shall be repaid together
with interest.   An application to the High Court or a
referee must be made within three months of the date of the
payment.   With respect to matters not covered by section
127, there is no right to recover except insofar as provided
by the common law.   However, an express discretion to repay
is given to the Commissioners by the section.

3.34   In practice, import duties are now collected only
on behalf of the European Community, and the recovery of the
amount of those duties which have been overpaid is governed
by specific Community legislation as is explained below.

(ix)   Charges Made by Public Utilities

3.35   Public utilities have often been subject to
statutory restrictions on the charges which they may make.
The companies authorised to supply gas and water following
the recent privatisation of these industries generally levy
their charges pursuant to statute and are subject to
statutory restrictions.[82]   No general provision has been

[82.] Water Act 1989, sections 75-82; Gas Act 1986, sections
12-14.

made for the recovery of amounts demanded in breach of these restrictions so it seems that the common law will normally apply. However there is a limited provision in the Water Act 1989: section 82(5) provides for recovery in the case where companies which are not "undertakers" within the Act provide water with the help of an undertaker and charge for it in excess of the amount prescribed under section 82.[83]

(x)   Fees Mistakenly Paid

3.36   There are also legislative provisions giving a right to the recovery of fees paid in return for the provision of goods and services, where an excess amount is paid. For example, the Land Registration Fees (No. 2) Order 1990, Article 9(1), gives a right to a refund "[w]here an amount exceeding the prescribed fee has been paid".[84] This would include excess payments made as a result of a mistake of law.

3.37   The practice of treating a power to make provision in subordinate legislation for payment of fees and charges

---

83. Where there is a breach of charging conditions in the company's licence, a person overcharged may obtain damages for any loss suffered if the company fails to comply with an order enforcing compliance with the conditions which might be used to claim the amount of an overpayment: Water Act 1989, sections 20-22.

84. An identical provision was made for repayment of overpaid fees in the Land Registration Fee Order 1988, Article 9. Following a challenge to the vires of a repayment provision in the Land Registry (Fees) Order (Northern Ireland) 1988 and the doubts expressed by the Joint Committee on Statutory Instruments (see para. 3.37 below), the repayment provision was not included in the Land Registration Fee Order 1990. It was reinstated following the introduction of section 128 of the Finance Act 1990.

as also conferring a power to make provisions for repayments was criticized by the Joint Committee on Statutory Instruments[85] but was validated for enactments then existing by section 128 of the Finance Act 1990. The effect of this is that where further enabling powers to make provision for the payment of fees and charges are taken, express provision in the primary legislation will now have to be made for repayments. The statutory provisions do not appear to affect the power to make a refund by way of an ex gratia payment.

(xi) The Relationship of the Legislative Structure and the General Restitutionary Principle

3.38   In Woolwich Equitable Building Society v. I.R.C. Butler-Sloss L.J. stated that significantly the legislative structure which governs taxation only provided for repayment of overpayments under intra vires regulations. "No structure is in place to deal with the demand for and payment of tax which has been unlawfully demanded under legislation found to be ultra vires. To deal with that eventuality the courts are thrown back upon the common law and precedent." It is not clear which statutes, if any, apart from the General Rate Act 1967[86] and the Taxes Management Act 1970[87] were before the Court. The argument that the legislative structure only deals with overpayments under intra vires regulations does not address the position of overpayments made directly under a statute where no regulations have been made. It is surely arguable that the statutory remedy applies whenever there has been payment of

---

85. 1988/89 H.C. 47-i.

86. See para. 3.17 above.

87. See para. 3.25 above.

a sum which, under the statute, is not due, although such payment in a sense is ultra vires.[88]   If so a somewhat unsatisfactory distinction would exist between payments by reason of an unauthorised demand not backed by regulations and payments by reason of an unauthorised demand contained in regulations.   Furthermore, it does not explain why statutory rights of recovery covering payments "by reason of a mistake",[89] where tax was "not tax due"[90] or, where "a lesser or no amount was properly payable"[91] are not appropriate to cover all relevant payments, whether intra vires or ultra vires.   Finally, the status of the limitations to statutory rights of recovery,[92] if there is a general common law right is uncertain.   Although section 24(7) of the Finance Act 1989 specifically states that there is to be no liability to repay V.A.T. by virtue of the fact that it was not tax due except under the section, other statutes are silent.

---

88. However, the reference in the Taxes Management Act 1970, section 33 to an "assessment" which "was excessive by reason of some error or mistake" could possibly be seen as confined to an assessment which, other than being excessive by reason of an error or mistake in the return, is for all other purposes final and conclusive and accordingly intra vires: see Simon's Taxes, Division A3.901.   Similar arguments could be made concerning the Stamp Act 1891, section 13(4) and the Inheritance Tax Act 1984, section 241.

89. Finance Act 1989, section 24(5), para. 3.21 above (V.A.T.).   See also ibid., section 29(2), para. 3.24 above (excise duty and car tax).

90. Finance Act 1989, section 24(1), para. 3.21 above (V.A.T.).

91. Customs and Excise Management Act 1979, section 127(2), para. 3.33.

92. See, for instance, paras. 3.22, 3.24, 3.25 and 3.27 above.

(c)   The Requirements of European Community Law

3.39   Alongside the "domestic" common law and statutory
rules, English law also contains rules relating to the
recovery of unlawfully levied charges which arise from
European Community law. These rules govern the recovery of
charges which are levied by domestic bodies in contravention
of Community law. Community law may be relevant; (i) where
charges are set by the U.K. government itself in
contravention of Community law and, (ii) where the U.K.
government collects on behalf of the Community charges which
have been set by the Community institutions.

(i)   Charges Set by the U.K. Government

3.40   A charge set by the United Kingdom government might
be invalid because it contravenes a rule of European law.
For example, Article 95 of the European Community Treaty,
prohibiting internal taxation which is discriminatory, has
been held to have direct effect on the legal relationship
between member states and those subject to their
jurisdiction and to create individual rights which national
courts must protect.[93]   Any action to recover the charge
will be brought against the Government in the domestic
courts.[94]   The rules and procedures of national law will
apply to the action for recovery, subject to the "principle
of effectiveness"; national law must provide a direct and
effective remedy to redress the breach of Community law.[95]

[93.] Case 28/67 Molkerei-Zentrale v. H.Z.A. Paderborn [1968]
E.C.R. 143.

[94.] This follows from the fact that none of the treaties
makes provision for an individual to sue a member state
in the European Court.

[95.] Case 33/76 Rewe v. Landwirtschaftskammer Saarland [1976]
E.C.R. 1989; Case 45/76 Comet v. Produktschap voor
Siergewassen [1976] E.C.R. 2043; Case 68/79

In connection with this principle, the European Court has stated that national rules must not make it "impossible in practice or excessively difficult" to exercise this remedy.[96]

3.41   These principles seem to require a prima facie rule permitting recovery of the unlawful charge from the government, regardless of whether or not the payment was made under a mistake.[97] It does not however, seem to be a requirement of the principle of effectiveness that interest be payable on the amount overpaid: this is probably a matter which is left to the choice of national law.[98] It is permissible for national law to provide for a defence of "unjust enrichment" of the payee[99] (and as it has been seen such a defence is contained in both sections 24 and 29 of the Finance Act 1989) although a requirement that the payer disprove the unjust enrichment has been held to be ineffective on the basis that this makes the exercise of this remedy too burdensome.[100] National law may also impose "reasonable" time limits on the exercise of the remedy.[101]

---

95. Continued
        Hans I/S Just v. Danish Ministry for Fiscal Affairs [1980] E.C.R. 501.

96.   Case 199/82 Amministrazione delle Finanze dello Stato v. SpA San Giorgio [1983] E.C.R. 3595.

97.   San Giorgio, ibid.

98.   Case 26/74 Roquette v. Commission [1976] E.C.R. 677.

99.   Just, op cit. The ruling has been criticised as contributing to the distortion of competition - see for example, Hubeau, [1985] C.M.L.R. 87; but it has been confirmed in many subsequent cases.

100.   San Giorgio, op cit.

101.   Rewe and Comet, op cit.

3.42   It has been explained that English law does not always provide a remedy for the recovery of charges which are invalid under domestic law. To the extent that the remedies under existing statutes do not accord with the above principles, in the case of a charge levied in breach of directly effective Community law, there are strong reasons within Community law that states accord a prima facie right of restitution in such cases. This is so even if no remedy would be given in a comparable domestic situation under the common law, for example because the sum was paid as a result of a mistake of law.

3.43   Community law also requires that any remedy for the recovery of charges invalid for breach of Community law must be at least as favourable as the remedy given for recovery in "similar" situations in domestic law.[102] Thus, to the extent that domestic law goes beyond the limited requirements of Community law, for example in allowing interest on repaid sums, those claiming sums paid in breach of Community law must be given the benefit of these provisions.

3.44   Most cases in which questions of restitution arise in connection with a breach of Community law involve authorities which are quite clearly regarded as being part of government. However, some provisions of Community law, are directed at bodies which might not traditionally be thought of as within the public sphere, such as public utilities which are privately owned but subject to a measure of state control.[103] It is possible that articles of the

---

102.   Rewe and Comet, op cit.

103.   Foster v. British Gas plc. [1991] 2 W.L.R. 258 (ECJ); [1991] 2 W.L.R. 1075 (H.L.).

treaty, such as those on discrimination, may even apply to bodies of a purely private nature which are profit making and subject to no state control or funding of any kind; but the case law in this area is still developing and it is not possible to say whether the European Court will go this far. It does seem clear, however, that in any case to which Community law does apply the requirement that a direct and effective remedy be available will also apply, regardless of the nature of the body in breach.

(ii)   Charges Collected on Behalf of the Community

3.45   The Community itself frequently levies charges on individuals: all customs duties on imports into member states are, for example, now set directly by the Community. Since the Community itself has no collection machinery, charges are collected on its behalf by the member states. The payer may seek to recover such a charge either because the levying provision is itself invalid as in breach of principles of Community administrative law (such as the principles of proportionality); or because the levying authority has misinterpreted the provision and levied a charge which is not within its scope.

3.46   In both cases any action for recovery must be brought against the collecting authority in the national courts.[104] According to general principles of Community law

---

104.   No action may be brought against the Community itself in respect of the amount unlawfully levied: cases 5,7 and 13-24/66 Kampffmeyer v. Commission [1967] E.C.R. 245; case 96/71 Haegeman v. Commission [1972] E.C.R. 1005. The case law is not entirely consistent and the current position has often been criticised. For discussion see Durdan, "Restitution or Damages: National Court or European Court?" (1975-6) 1 E.L.Rev. 431; Hartley, "Concurrent Liability in EEC Law: A Critical

D

the action is governed by the rules and procedure of national law.[105] Although the European Court does not appear explicitly to have ruled on this point, the action is probably here also subject to the principles of effectiveness and non-discrimination. In practice the question is, however, probably academic, since the matter is specifically dealt with by Council Regulation 1430/1979 which gives a general right to the recovery of such charges,[106] and appears to leave little room for the operation of national law.

(d)   Procedure

3.47   Where recovery is allowed either under statute or a private law ground for restitution, such as mistake of fact or duress, it seems that the ordinary writ procedure will apply. Where recovery is based on the invalidity of the demand the position is less clear. An action for recovery of an invalid tax does not seem to fall within the special procedure for "public law" actions contained in Order 53 and in section 31 of the Supreme Court Act 1981, since the provisions apply only to damages claims and not to actions

---

104.   Continued
            Review of the Cases" (1977) 2 E.L.Rev. 249;
            Harding, "The Choice of Court Problem in Cases of
            Non-Contractual Liability under E.E.C. Law" (1979)
            16 C.M.L.R. 389; Lewis, "Joint and Several
            Liability of the European Communities and National
            Authorities" (1980) C.L.P. 99;   Oliver, "Joint
            Liability of the Community and the Member States",
            Ch. 10 in Non-Contractual Liability of the European
            Communities (1988) ed. Schermers, Heukels and Mead.

105.   Haegeman v. Commisssion, ibid.

106.   Article 2.   Similar provisions will eventually be
            incorporated in the Customs Code which is currently
            being drafted.

in restitution.[107]   In the Woolwich case the building
society had, before bringing the civil action for
restitution, obtained a declaration that the demand was
unlawful in judicial review proceedings.[108]   There were
indications in the judgments of Glidewell and Ralph Gibson
L.JJ. that judicial review proceedings may be a necessary
preliminary to the civil action, although no concluded view
was expressed.[109]   Cases, such as Woolwich, where recovery
is based on the invalidity of the demand, may be held not to
fall within the O'Reilly v. Mackman exclusivity principle
that normally requires public law rights to be asserted by
the application for judicial review. This may be for one of
two reasons: first, because of the absence of provision for
restitutionary relief under Order 53 and the undesirability
of requiring two sets of proceedings and secondly, because
the exclusivity principle does not apply. The fact that the
right only arises in respect of payments to public
authorities is not conclusive since, for example, there is
no suggestion that proceedings for the tort of misfeasance
in public office must be brought under Order 53.[110]

---

107.   See Wandsworth L.B.C. v. Winder [1985] A.C. 461,
        484 per Parker L.J. Robert Goff L.J. (at p. 480)
        stated emphatically that there was no power to
        award restitution on an application for judicial
        review.

108.   R. v. I.R.C.,Ex p. Woolwich Equitable Building
        Society [1990] 1 W.L.R. 1400.

109.   See the O'Reilly v. Mackman [1983] 2 A.C. 237
        exclusivity principle and Cocks v. Thanet D.C.
        [1983] 2 A.C. 286 (public law remedy in effect held
        to be a condition precedent to the statutory
        private law right of a homeless person to be
        accommodated) but cf. Wandsworth L.B.C. v. Winder
        [1985] A.C. 461, 508 (per Lord Fraser of
        Tullybelton).

110.   Bourgoin S.A. v. Ministry of Agriculture, Fisheries
        & Food [1986] Q.B. 716. Given the origins of the
        general restitutionary principle generating the
        right of recovery, the "collateral issue" exception
        to the exclusivity principle may apply. See H.W.R.
        Wade, Administrative Law (6th ed., 1988), pp.
        686-687.

2.   THE CASE FOR REFORM

3.48   It has been explained that in the case of payments
made pursuant to an invalid demand by a public authority the
fact that the payments were made as a result of a mistake of
law is generally insufficient to ground recovery.   This is
so both on the traditional approach and the newly enunciated
general restitutionary principle.   Although in many cases
there is a statutory right to recover such payments, in
others the citizen will be unable to recover.

3.49   The arguments put forward in Part II of this paper
for the reform of the general mistake of law rule apply
equally in the context of public authorities. Firstly, and
fundamentally, the payment which enriches the public
authority payee is non-voluntary if made in the mistaken
belief that it was lawfully due under statute and
consequently the enrichment is prima facie unjust.

3.50   Secondly, the current rules seem arbitrary and
anomalous, failing to treat what appear to be like cases in
a like manner.   As in the private sphere, this position
arises from the fact that mistakes of law are treated
differently from mistakes of fact, and also from the
existence of exceptions to the general mistake of law rule,
both under statute and under the common law, which mean that
even all cases of mistake of law are not treated alike,
though without any apparent justification.[111]   In the

---

111.   A particular anomaly has been said to arise under
the traditional approach with respect to the
alleged exception for payments made in return for
the performance of a public duty. Where a payment
is made for the issue of a licence it will be
recoverable if there is a duty to issue such a
licence without payment of a fee; but if the whole
scheme is invalid and no licence could be required
at all, there will be no duty to issue the licence

public sphere, once a general restitutionary principle based
on broad considerations of justice is recognised, the
continued irrecoverability of payments made under a mistake
of law is, as Glidewell L.J. recognised, arguably
illogical.[112] We have seen that the unsatisfactory nature of
this distinction was an important factor in Ralph Gibson
L.J.'s dissenting judgment[113] and the constitutional
argument based on the Bill of Rights[114] appears equally
applicable to payments under mistake of law. Furthermore,
the statutory inroads into the common law have been
piecemeal and there is a case for rationalizing these
developments so as to simplify the law in this area. It may
also be necessary to allow recovery where there is a
mistaken payment because of the requirements of European
Community law, thus creating a further apparent anomaly in
the treatment of similar cases.

3.51   Finally, the law in this area is as uncertain and
complex as in the private sphere, if not more so.   As
elsewhere, uncertainty is caused by the various
qualifications and exceptions to the principle of recovery,
whether based on the traditional approach or a general
public law restitutionary right.   We have seen that it is
not clear whether the mistake of law limitation on the
general principle of recovery enunciated in the Woolwich

---

111.   Continued
        and so no recovery. (See the dissent of McTiernan
        J in Mason v. New South Wales (1959) 102 C.L.R.
        108).   Thus recovery is refused in the case of
        greater illegality.

112.   Glidewell L.J. said that the "closing the
        transaction" limitation to the general principle
        might also be illogical.

113.   See para. 3.15 above.

114.   See para. 3.14 above.

E

case applies only to the mistaken construction of a statute, or whether it extends to a mistake of law as to the vires of a regulation or to all mistakes of law.[115]

3.52   Uncertainty also results from the application of the fact-law distinction. It is interesting that many of the cases on the nature of the distinction have concerned the application of statutes or regulations where it has been necessary to determine the scope of particular statutory descriptions.[116] In this context, as others, the distinction and the exceptions to the rule are also open to manipulation to produce justice in individual cases, for example, by a willingness to imply a contract to repay or by construing a mistake as to the existence of a valid by-law as a mistake of fact.[117]   One of the clearest indications of judicial dislike of the rule, already mentioned,[118] was given in the context of an overpayment of tax.   In Sebel Products Ltd. v. Commissioners of Customs and Excise Vaisey J., after acknowledging that the Crown was strictly entitled to and could in appropriate cases properly refuse to refund tax paid under a mistake of law, stated that "... the defence is one which ought to be used with great discretion ..." because, inter alia the Crown, as the source and fountain of justice, should maintain the highest standards of probity and fair dealing.[119]

---

115.   See para. 3.13 above.

116.   e.g. Holt v. Markham [1923] 1 K.B. 504.

117.   George (Porky) Jacobs Enterprises Ltd. v. City of Regina, [1964] S.C.R. 326, discussed in para. 2.22 above.

118.   See para. 2.23 above.

119.   [1949] Ch. 409, 413. For the practice which has grown up as a consequence, see para. 2.23 above.

3.53   If the House of Lords affirms the general restitutionary principle enunciated in the _Woolwich_ case the case for reform is primarily one of eliminating any remaining unsatisfactory limitations to the principle (they would not necessarily be bound by the mistake of law rule) and rationalising the statutory rights of recovery in the light of it.   Ralph Gibson L.J.'s conclusion[120] that there is no general principle was based on the public interest and the existence of legislation which appears to assume that there is no general right of recovery [121] and which subjects statutory rights to prudential limitations.   These considerations may incline their Lordships to find that the traditional approach represents the existing law whatever the arguments favouring the introduction of a general right of recovery.[122] In that event the question of whether the law should be reformed to accord a general right of recovery for payments made in response to an ultra vires demand arises.   We therefore set out the arguments concerning such a right, many of which were considered in the _Woolwich_ case.

3.54   The arguments accepted in the _Woolwich_ case are that public authorities are in a special position and should be expected to behave with higher standards of fairness and equity towards others than should private individuals and that it is ultra vires for the public authority to receive the payment and consequently to retain it.   It is the constitutional principle of ultra vires and the importance of Parliamentary intention rather than the involuntariness of the payment that has been emphasised as a reason for

---

120.   Para. 3.15 above.

121.   See para. 3.38 above for Butler-Sloss L.J.'s treatment of this.

122.   For a full exposition of the arguments see para. 3.14 above and the literature cited in para. 3.61 below.

giving a remedy in this area.[123]   A number of practical
arguments also favour recovery. A rule permitting recovery
gives an authority an incentive to avoid making any ultra
vires demands, and, in the authority's favour, it may
encourage the prompt payment of taxes and charges.[124]

3.55   A second argument stems from the different
treatment of payments to public authorities and payments by
public authorities. It will be seen in Part IV that the
public authority which makes an ultra vires payment has the
benefit of a special rule permitting recovery while, as we
have seen, the traditional approach gives the public
authority which receives an ultra vires payment the benefit
of the ordinary rule precluding recovery. Although the
justification of the special protection of public authority
payers, that of protecting public funds from unlawful
dissipation, does not apply to receipts by public
authorities, the overall imbalance is distinctly
unattractive and we have seen that other principles suggest
that it is unjustified.

3.56   The current position has also been said to favour
those with greater resources and better access to legal
advice, and those who are more prone to dispute their
liabilities, particularly if restitutionary proceedings must
be preceded by judicial review. Furthermore, the authority
is normally in the best position to know the scope of its
powers and thus to avoid making an ultra vires demand.

---

123.   This argument has been emphasised particularly by
         Birks in the works cited in para. 3.61 below and
         was relied on in   Woolwich Equitable Building
         Society v. I.R.C. The Times, 27 May 1991.

124.   Sebel Products Ltd. v. Commissioners of Customs and
         Excise [1949] Ch. 409.

Although it is true that the payer's fault in making a mistake is not generally relevant in the private sphere this may be a relevant factor in this context. Finally, it is argued that recovery is likely to increase public confidence in the fairness of government.

3.57   However, although it is acknowledged that there may be particularly strong arguments favouring recovery in this context it has often been suggested that the counter-arguments are stronger. Particular concern has been expressed about the potential for disruption to public finances if a wide right of recovery were to be given,[125] a specific manifestation of the general concern with security of receipts which has been said to justify the general irrecoverability of payments made under a mistake of law[126] and the limitations placed upon statutory rights of recovery.[127] The general principle stated in the Woolwich case was not made subject to any limitations reflecting this concern. We provisionally consider that reform, whether by way of the introduction of a general right, if the traditional approach prevails, or through the refinement of the general principle in Woolwich, should address this concern.

3.58   The general consensus of commentators and of law reform bodies has been that the best balance between public

---

125.   Glasgow Corporation v. Lord Advocate 1959 S.C. 203; Air Canada v. British Columbia [1989] 1 S.C.R. 1161. See paras. 3.70-3.73 below. These concerns were expressed by Ralph Gibson L.J. in the Woolwich case, para. 3.15 above.

126.   See paras. 2.34-2.35 above.

127.   See paras. 3.22, 3.24, 3.25 and 3.27 above.

and private interests is obtained by a general rule providing for recovery, rather than by one which precludes recovery altogether.[128] Although there are differences as to the nature and extent of the restrictions which ought to be placed on the right to recover, it is our provisional view that there is a good case for a general right of recovery but subject to such restrictions as may be considered desirable in the public interest. The discussion which follows will proceed on this basis, examining the possible approaches to reform and considering secondly the question of restrictions to any right of recovery.

3.   OPTIONS FOR REFORM

(a)   Abrogation of the Mistake of Law Rule

3.59   One possible option for reform is simply to follow the approach we have provisionally recommended in Part II of this paper and to abrogate the mistake of law rule by assimilating the position to that of payments made under a mistake of fact.   On this approach there would be no need for separate treatment of ultra vires payments (except insofar as special defences might be considered apposite) since the general provision recommended above would apply to such payments.   This appears to be the position in Canada[129]

---

128.   See paras. 3.61, 3.73 below.

129.   Air Canada v. British Columbia [1989] 1 S.C.R. 1161. Lamer, La Forest and L' Heureux-Dube JJ who favoured abrogation of the general mistake of law rule, would have barred recovery of unconstitutional and ultra vires levies because of the danger of disruption to public finances. The majority considered the general principle enabling restitution of mistaken payments applied to constitutional or intra vires legislation which was misapplied or misinterpreted. Wilson J., while favouring abrogation of the rule, would allow recovery of all taxes not lawfully due where

98

and is the law recommended for New South Wales.[130] It has also been adopted in the U.K. in respect of overpaid car tax and excise duty.[131] An advantage of applying the ordinary rules of recovery, is that no distinction need be made in this context between public and private law. This distinction is a complex one[132] and could well lead to uncertainty. Another possible advantage is that no general principle of statutory recovery need be formulated, since the law is left to develop by analogy with the common law governing mistake of fact. However, in many of the cases it is difficult to characterise the facts as involving a mistake. If recovery is only allowed where the excess payment is caused by a mistake the courts may continue to facilitate recovery in the event of an ultra vires levy, either by a wide interpretation of "mistake" or by a "generous" application of other private law grounds, as is seen now in relation to the implication of a threat so as to establish duress or of a contract to repay. It might thus be doubted whether such an approach would have any real advantages in terms of producing certainty and it does not address the constitutional argument.

---

129.   Continued
        made under a mistake of law. Beetz and McIntyre
        JJ. did not express any view on the mistake of law
        rule, but considered that if recovery were
        generally to be allowed for mistake of law it
        should extend to misapplication of the law.

130.   Restitution of Benefits Conferred under Mistake of
        Law LCR 53 (1987), pp. 64-66 (the possibility of a
        special rule based simply on the unlawful nature of
        the demand was not considered).

131.   Discussed at para. 3.24 above.

132.   e.g. Administrative Justice - Some Necessary
        Reforms Justice - All Souls Review of
        Administrative Law in the UK (1988), pp. 150ff.;
        H.W.R Wade, Administrative Law (6th ed., 1988),
        p.938.

(b)   Recovery of ultra vires payments

3.60   An alternative approach for which there is much
support is to build on the approach of the majority in the
Woolwich case. This would be to recognise a rule allowing
for recovery from public authorities to be based simply on
the unlawful nature of the levy, whether or not the payer
was mistaken.   The basis of a general restitutionary
principle in public law cases is set out in paragraph 3.14.
Even Ralph Gibson L.J., while not accepting it as the
present law, said that if reform of the law was being
considered, he would start with a preference in favour of
the law being based on a prima facie right of recovery.
Some existing legislation gives a right to recover based
simply on the unlawful nature of the levy; for example
provisions on V.A.T., the Community Charge and Rates and
also those on Inheritance Tax.[133] It seems inconsistent to
allow a right of recovery based solely on invalidity in
these cases, whilst requiring proof of mistake in others.
European Community law also provides a general right to
recover a charge levied contrary to its provisions,
regardless of whether or not the payment has been made as a
result of a mistake.

3.61   The view taken by the majority in the Woolwich case
that there should be a right to recover overpaid taxes based
simply on the fact of overpayment is one which has been put
forward by many commentators.[134] The Justice - All Souls

---

133.   For the limits on recovery of Inheritance Tax, see
         para. 3.27 above.

134.   Birks, "Restitution from the Executive: a
         Tercentenary Footnote to the Bill of Rights" in
         Essays on Restitution (ed., Finn, 1990), Ch. 6;
         Cornish, "Colour of Office: Restitutionary Redress
         against Public Authority" [1987] J.Mal.& Comp.L.
         41. Others have also argued for a right of

Review of Administrative Law in the UK[135] and the Law Reform Commission of British Columbia[136] also recommended this approach. The arguments supporting a right of recovery (the special constitutional position of public authorities, deterrence of ultra vires levies and encouragement of prompt payment) suggest that what is needed is a general right against public authority payees, rather than, as in the case of private law, one based on the circumstances of the payer. A disadvantage of this approach as compared to one affording recovery for "mistake of law" is, as indicated, the need to specify the type of bodies and payments to which the rule should apply. Statutory reform on these lines is likely to involve more elaborate legislation than reform based on mistake since it would require the identification and solution of a number of problems.[137] It has been seen that this may be avoided if reform is based on mistake since reference can be made to the common law principles governing recovery for mistake of fact.

---

134. Continued

recovery based on the unlawful nature of the demand but subject to limitations. See, for example: Collins, "Restitution from Government Officials" (1984) 29 McGill LJ 407; McKenna, "Mistake of Law Between Statutory Bodies and Private Citizens" (1979) 37 U.of T. Fac. L. Rev. 223; Pannam, "The Recovery of Unconstitutional Taxes in Australia and the United States" (1964) 42 Texas LR 777. Craig, Administrative Law (2nd ed., 1989), p.468, argues for a wide right of recovery but seems to assume this would be achieved by a liberal application of the private law.

135. Administrative Justice: Some Necessary Reforms (1988) p. 363.

136. Report on Benefits Conferred under a Mistake of Law LRC No. 51 (1981) pp. 84-88.

137. These include; disruption to public finances paras. 3.70-3.73 below); payments in accordance with the prevailing general practice (paras. 3.74-3.75 below); compromises or submissions to claims

3.62   The importance of the difference between these two approaches depends to a large extent on the meaning of mistake in this context. This has not been much considered in English law, perhaps because the mistake of law rule precludes recovery regardless of the existence of mistake in most cases. Any attempt to define mistake must consider the circumstances in which a payer who has doubts about his liability to pay will not be considered to be labouring under a mistake but rather to have taken the risk, as where he pays following a claim the validity of which he doubts. It is sufficient in this context to state that some doubt will not automatically preclude recovery for mistake,[138] although the exact measure of doubt that will result in the payment being regarded as "voluntary" is unclear. However, there comes a point at which a court will consider that a payer who pays in spite of his doubt has waived all inquiry into the circumstances.   Such a payer will be held to have intended the payee to have the money in any event.[139]

3.63   It has been suggested that a party can still be said to be mistaken in spite of serious doubts as to the validity of the claim where he pays believing that it is possible that there is a valid basis for the claim.[140] If this is so there would be little difference in practice

---

137.   Continued
        (paras. 3.65-3.69 below); defences such as change of position or estoppel (paras. 3.77-3.78 below); special limitation periods for public authorities (para. 3.79 below).

138.   See Goff and Jones, p.105n; Chatfield v. Paxton (1802) 2 East. 471 n(a).

139.   Kelly v. Solari (1841) 9 M. & W. 54, 59.   See paras. 2.2 above, 3.65-3.67 below.

140.   Palmer, pp. 166-174; Woolwich Equitable Building Society v. I.R.C. The Times, 27 May 1991 (per Ralph Gibson L.J.).

between the two approaches. The general restitutionary principle in public law cases would only have a distinct operation where the payer pays in the firm belief that the money is not owed. In a case where there are serious doubts it is arguable that recovery should be precluded anyway on the basis that there has been a waiver, or a submission to or a compromise of a disputed claim, i.e. the payment is made to close the transaction.[141] However, if a narrow approach to mistake were to be adopted by the common law a general restitutionary principle in public law cases would be important. It could apply in circumstances where a payer's doubts about liability sufficed to preclude recovery for mistake, but did not amount to waiver, compromise of, or submission to the authority's claim. It would also have significance if the arguments of those who consider that the submission and compromise rules should not apply or should apply in a restricted way to payments made in response to an ultra vires claim of a public authority are accepted.[142]

3.64   As there may be many cases of dispute where mere payment is not held to amount to a compromise or submission and the scope of mistake at common law is uncertain we incline to the view that the preferred option is to have a special rule of recovery for ultra vires payments, rather than to rely on the mistake approach. However, in view of the difficulties with this particularly in defining the scope of a special rule, we would appreciate the views of consultees as to the relative merits of this approach and the alternative of abrogating the mistake of law rule in this as well as in the private law context.

---

141.   See para. 3.65 below.

142.   See paras. 3.67-3.69 below.

4. SOME SPECIFIC DIFFICULTIES

(a)   A Defence of Submission to an Honest Claim?

3.65   The fact that the payment is made in submission to
an honest claim has been stated to constitute a defence to a
restitutionary action based on mistake of fact, and would
likewise be a defence to an action based on mistake of law
if the rules on recovery for mistake of law were to be
assimilated to those governing mistake of fact.   If the
general restitutionary principle enunciated in the Woolwich
case is affirmed without modification, a payment to close a
transaction although made pursuant to an ultra vires levy,
will be irrecoverable.   It is, however, necessary to
consider whether this should be so in the context of
payments to public authorities, whether the right to recover
is based on mistake or simply on the ultra vires nature of
the levy.

3.66   The historical origins of the submission and
compromise rules differ in that the former developed from
the principle that a judgment is conclusive between the
parties which eventually included submission to claims at
all stages of an action.   This has sometimes been referred
to as the "process of law" doctrine.   Compromise is a
contractual doctrine which originally only applied to valid
claims.[143]   The distinction was obscured when invalid claims
were brought within the compromise rule.[144]   The phrase
"submission to an honest claim" is also used to refer to a
principle stated in Kelly v. Solari; that there may be no
recovery where a payer intends "to waive all inquiry...

---

143.   See Beatson, [1974] C.L.J. 97.

144.   Longridge v. Dorville (1821) 5 B. & Ald. 117; Haigh
v. Brooks (1839) 10 Ad. & E. 309.   The leading case
is Callisher v. Bischoffsheim (1870) L.R. 5 Q.B.
449.

and that the person receiving shall have the money at all events."[145] It is not clear whether in modern law the idea of submission to an honest claim is just another word for a contractual settlement (or compromise), or whether it provides a separate defence[146] capable of applying even where there cannot be said to have been contractual agreement. If the two are separate the extent to which the "process of law" doctrine and the limitation based on waiver envisaged in Kelly v. Solari are separate principles is also unclear. As far as problems other than that of invalid levies by public authorities are concerned, this question will be left to the common law if measures are taken to assimilate mistake of law to mistake of fact as has been provisionally recommended in Part II. This is desirable in view of the wide variety of different fact situations which might occur.

3.67   In the specific context of invalid charges, on the other hand, it is our view that, if the basis of recovery is the invalidity of the charge, in principle there is a case for permitting recovery in all cases falling short of contractual compromise. Subject to what emerges on consultation, taking account of the special factors favouring recovery set out in paragraphs 3.54-3.56 above, and assuming that there are no special problems (such as the difficulties of defining public law) making a general right to recovery inappropriate, there seems to be no reason to

---

145.   (1841) 9 M. & W. 54, 59.

146.   It is argued by Andrews that there is no difference between the two: "Mistaken Settlements of Disputable Claims" [1989] L.M.C.L.Q. 431.

deny recovery of an invalid charge in the absence of any contract or estoppel to the contrary.[147]

3.68   The question of contractual compromise itself is more problematic. Under the general law it is normally open to a party to compromise a disputed legal claim whether based on a statutory or common law right and a payer could accordingly agree to forgo any statutory right which he has to recover an ultra vires payment. Clearly he will be unable to recover where there is an express agreement to this effect, for example, where he agrees to pay by way of compromise only part of the amount which it is alleged is owed. However, it may be that there can also be said to be a contractual compromise where the full amount is paid in order to avoid a legal action. An exception to this might be the case of European law. Where a claim is based on a breach of European law, the European Court of Justice might not uphold any compromise of the claim where this would prejudice the policy of the relevant Community provisions. Thus, to refuse recovery of a discriminatory customs charge because it has been paid to avoid a legal action would infringe the policy of promoting fair competition, and this consideration might override the public authority's interests. The Court has not, however, ruled specifically on this point.

3.69   It might be argued that the importance of the principle of legality is such that the right to recover such overpayments should also be absolute in domestic law, and should not be barred by the fact that the payer made the

---

147.   In Woolwich Equitable Building Society v. I.R.C. The Times, 27 May 1991, Ralph Gibson L.J. appeared in sympathy with this approach.

payment in order to avoid a lawsuit. It has also been suggested that public authorities do not need the same protection of their receipts as private individuals and hence do not need the protection given by the power to enter into compromises with the taxpayer.[148] Moreover, the concept of an "implied" compromise could be used by the courts to weaken substantially the impact of a special recovery rule in cases where the amount of the payment is not disputed. However, we are of the view that the right to compromise a claim with a public authority ought to be maintained where it is done clearly. There are obvious practical advantages in managerial powers to make a binding compromise and frequently compromises are entered into by the Revenue under section 54 of the Taxes Management Act 1970. However, principle also supports the ability of public authorities to compromise claims. The public interest in avoiding litigation is as important in the context of tax claims and other claims by public authorities as in other contexts.

(b)　　　The Problem of Disruption to Public Finance[149]

3.70　　　An objection often made to any rule allowing recovery of invalid charges on a wide scale, whether based on mistake of law or the ultra vires nature of the levy, is that the need for security of receipts is particularly strong in this context, and that a rule which allows recovery might lead to serious disruption of public finances. As with any other individual, expenditures by the authority is made on the basis of anticipated receipts, and if a levy is made which is invalid and must be returned,

---

148.　　　Cornish, [1987] J.Mal.& Comp.L. 41, 51-52.

149.　　　This is a distinct issue from the general concern of security of receipts, on which see para. 2.34 above.

this may have the effect of reducing receipts on a large scale.

3.71   When a large number of payments must be returned the expenditure has to be recouped by the authority either by raising more revenue in a different manner, or by cutting expenditure in the future. Injustice may result from the manner in which this is done. The authority may be unable to reproduce the position which it would have wished for had it known of the illegality originally, since the group of potential payers is unlikely to be identical to the previous group, and it will not be possible to reverse expenditure already made. Thus a totally different group of taxpayers may end up paying either directly, or indirectly, through a cut in services for past expenditure. This might be exacerbated by the fact that it is sought to raise in a short time revenue to replace that which had been acquired in the past over a much longer period, so that the burden could fall on a smaller group. The effect of allowing recovery is not always to redistribute the "loss" amongst a wider group.[150] It is not at all obvious that to allow recovery is automatically a fairer solution than to leave the burden on those on whom it originally rested, albeit illegally.

3.72   The difficulty in dealing with this type of problem is that it varies enormously from case to case. Its significance depends on such factors as; (a) the effect of recovery on the authority's total revenue, which in turn depends on the nature of the error, and the overall

---

150.   Wilson J. in her dissenting judgment in Air Canada v. British Columbia [1989] 1 S.C.R. 1161 thought that granting recovery of taxes levied pursuant to unconstitutional legislation would have this effect.

significance of the particular source of revenue and, (b) the length of time which has elapsed since the payments were made. The potentially wide variation of circumstances makes it difficult to draw up any single rule which would be entirely satisfactory.

3.73   In the majority of cases, however, we believe that it will be fairer to allow recovery than to refuse it. This is particularly so in the case of central government where revenue is collected from a wide variety of sources and the benefits of expenditure are widely dispersed. It is for this reason we provisionally suggest, as have the majority of law reform agencies and commentators, that the presumptive rule should be one favouring recovery rather than denying it. However, the question still remains as to whether this presumptive rule should be limited to deal with the problem of disruption to public finances. There are a number of possible ways of dealing with the problem without refusing to allow recovery in all cases.

Payments Made in accordance with General Practice

3.74   One way of dealing with disruption to public finances might be by discriminating between different types of invalid decisions. This approach has been adopted in a number of statutory rights of recovery, in particular Income Tax and Corporation Tax, Capital Gains Tax, Petroleum Revenue Tax and Inheritance Tax which preclude recovery of charges levied in accordance with general practice.[151]   To the extent that such provisions preclude recovery where there has been a change in the understanding of the law

---

151.   For a discussion of the statutory provisions allowing for recovery see paras. 3.20 et seq. above.

F

because of a judicial decision they are in line with what we consider should be the position under the general law.[152] However, the legislation has been interpreted in a manner which goes beyond this. It has been held, in the context of the General Rate Act 1967, that a provision of this kind applied even though the authority's interpretation of the provision was "demonstrably wrong" at the time.[153] There is also support for the view that a "general practice" is one which the revenue authorities have adopted in the past.[154] It is thus sufficient that the payment is made in accordance with the general practice which has been set by the authority's own demands.

3.75 Although a rule which makes the right to recover a payment depend on whether it is an isolated case or one of many which are similar is better than refusing recovery altogether, it appears rather a blunt instrument for dealing with the problem of disruption to public finance.

No Retrospective Effect

3.76 Another way of seeking to meet fears that a right of recovery would disrupt public finances is to restrict recovery to those who had instituted proceedings before the

---

152.   See para. 2.58 above.

153.   R. v. Richmond upon Thames L.B.C., Ex p. Stubbs (1989) 87 L.G.R. 637.

154.   Murray's Trustees v. Lord Advocate 1959 S.C. 400, 415. Whether the "general practice" restriction applies where the Revenue is demonstrably wrong in its interpretation does not seem to have been discussed specifically in the cases, but see Stopforth, "Error or Mistake Relief" (1989) 5 B.T.R. 151 and note that the determination of what constitutes general practice is a question of fact for the Special Commissioners.

determination that the payment was invalid.   Although not a technique that has been used by the courts in England, it has been used in this context by the European Court of Justice[155] and the Supreme Court of Ireland.[156] The former case concerned university fees which were held to be discriminatory on grounds of nationality and the European Court of Justice stated that "pressing considerations of legal certainty preclude any re-opening of the question of past legal relationships where that would retroactively throw the financing of university education into confusion and might have unforeseeable consequences for the proper functioning of universities".[157]   A similar technique is utilized in clause 50 of the Finance Bill 1991.   The proposed legislation seeks to rectify the invalidity of the Income Tax (Building Societies) Regulations 1986 as held by the House of Lords in R v. I.R.C., Ex parte Woolwich Equitable Building Society.[158]   However, the proposals expressly provide that the section is not to apply in relation to a building society which commenced proceedings to challenge the validity of the regulations before 18th July 1986.

---

155.   Case 24/86 Blaizot v. University of Liege [1989] 1 C.M.L.R. 57.

156.   Murphy v. Attorney-General [1982] 1 I.R. 241, 324 (cf. O'Higgins C.J. and Kenny J., ibid., 301-302, 335-336).

157.   Case 24/86 Blaizot v. University of Liege [1989] 1 C.M.L.R. 57, 69 (n.b. one circumstance leading the court to this conclusion was the conduct of the European Commission which might have led the Belgian authorities to consider that their legislation conformed to Community law).

158.   [1990] 1 W.L.R. 1400.   In the absence of this provision the cost to the government of repayment, including accumulated interest, has been said to be in the order of £250 million; Hansard (H.C.) 4 June 1991, Vol. 192, 140-1. (Written Answers to Questions).

Change of Position Defence

3.77   A change of position defence is another possible limitation to a right of recovery against public authorities. This would apply when expenditure had been made on the basis of the receipts but its effect would depend on the courts' approach towards proof of reliance on the receipts. While government generally tailors its expenditure in some way to its receipts, it would be difficult to show that a particular expenditure would not have been incurred but for the receipts. Proof of reliance would be particularly difficult in relation to taxation and the expenditure of central government. In Canada it has been held that the defence can only be invoked where a link can be shown between a specific receipt and a specific item of expenditure,[159] something which is very difficult to do in many cases, particularly for a public authority. The reason for this strict approach would seem to be to avoid a very complex factual investigation. The difficulties of proof suggest that even if this were in principle an appropriate method to deal with the special problems faced by public authorities it might not be an adequate one. It is, however, possible that the broad formulation of the defence in <u>Lipkin Gorman</u> v. <u>Karpnale Ltd.</u>,[160] under which the overall position rather than the position after individual payments was considered, will mean that it can be invoked by governmental bodies.

---

159.   <u>Rural Municipality of Storthoaks</u> v. <u>Mobil Oil Canada Ltd</u>. [1976] 2 S.C.R. 147; <u>Hydro Electric Commission of the Township of Nepean</u> v. <u>Ontario Hydro</u> [1982] 1 S.C.R. 347.

160.   Para. 2.68 above.

3.78   However, it may be questioned whether such a defence is desirable in principle where the burden of repaying will be redistributed by the public authority whether by subsequent intra vires taxation or by other means.   The defence is not directed at the particular problems of public authorities and where it applies the defence automatically shifts the net loss from "future" generations of tax or charge payers to those who suffered from the illegal levy.   It does not appear to us that this is an appropriate result.   No such defence is provided in any of the statutory provisions conferring a right to recovery of charges not due.   The complexity of the factual determinations which it would involve in this context also suggest that it should not be adopted.   It is our provisional view that not only would a defence of change of position not be particularly helpful in dealing with the problem of disruption to public finance but it should not be available at all.   However, again we would welcome comments from consultees.

Short Limitation Periods

3.79   At common law a claim in restitution for a payment not due may normally be brought within six years of the payment, or, where the claim is based on mistake, within six years from the time that the mistake ought to have been discovered.[161]   An alternative way of dealing with the problem of disruption to public finance is by providing shorter time limits for recovery.   The effect of this is to reduce the potential effect of any disruption by minimising the overall amount recoverable.   By allowing recovery only for a short period the potential inequity of redistributing

---

161.   McLean, "Limitation of Actions in Restitution" [1989] C.L.J. 472, 476, 479.

the burden amongst a different group is also minimised. A limitation period which has these effects but also provides a reasonable opportunity for a payer to dispute the validity of a charge and to take action seems to be an acceptable solution to the problem where it is likely to arise. It is, however, not suggested that shorter limitation periods should be prescribed for all public law claims: in most cases there would be no reason to depart from the ordinary six year rule. The current provisions concerning the recovery of income tax, V.A.T., excise duty and import duties are subject to the ordinary limitation period.[162] There are indications in the <u>Woolwich</u> case that a necessary precondition to recovery is that the invalidity of the demand be established in judicial review proceedings although no concluded view was expressed. If this turns out to be a requirement the very short three month limitation period will apply.[163] It may, however, be that the ordinary limitation period would be appropriate for many cases concerning central governmental authorities and bodies levying charges pursuant to statute. There is, on the other hand, an argument for a shorter period applying to charges levied by local authorities and others such as public utilities with more limited sources of revenue and a more limited tax base in order to achieve a fair balance between the position of those who have been required to pay unlawful charges and those on whom the burden would fall if the charges would be recoverable within the ordinary limitation period. Provision for shorter limitation periods could be

---

162.   Taxes Management Act 1970, section 33; Finance Act 1989, sections 24(4); Customs and Excise Management Act 1979, section 17(5). Repayment under the Taxes Management Act 1970, section 33 (see para. 3.25 above) is not of particular significance since the basic right to recover is fairly narrow.

163.   Supreme Court Act 1981, section 31(6); R.S.C. Order 53, r. 4.

made in legislation which would identify the bodies to which they would apply. The Law Reform Commission of British Columbia recommended a two year limitation period for actions against municipal authorities,[164] and this seems to provide a reasonable balance between the conflicting interests involved.

Legislation Precluding Recovery

3.80   A final point in relation to the problem of disruption to public finances is that where serious disruption does occur legislation may be passed to preclude recovery to the extent that this is felt necessary.[165] This possibility may not be particularly pertinent in relation to local authorities and other bodies which do not have the power to legislate and whose predicament may not be of sufficient concern to central government to warrant the effort of legislation. It is, however, a significant factor in relation to bodies whose finances are more closely associated with the central government and may be some support for the application of the normal limitation period to payments to central government bodies.

(c)   "Passing On"

3.81   Another issue to consider in respect of the recovery of invalid charges is where the burden of a charge

---

164.   LRC 51, pp. 84-88.

165.   See, for example, clause 50 of the Finance Bill 1991 discussed in para. 3.76 above, although this has proved controversial, see the correspondence in The Times, 15, 17, 21 May 1991. Cf. the decision not to legislate to validate "swaps" transactions, which also attracted comment, e.g. City Comment, Daily Telegraph, 8 May 1991.

has effectively been "passed on" to other parties by the charge payer through an increase in the price of goods or services to take account of the higher cost to the payer arising from the payment of the charge. This may occur where a charge is levied which relates directly to specific goods or services such as V.A.T. or import or export charges levied on particular items, in which case the whole amount of the charge may be directly added to the price of the goods or services. It might also occur in the context of overpaid corporation tax where it could be argued that the price of a firm's product had been increased to reflect the tax paid. A defence of "passing on" could in theory be raised in any action for restitution where the diminishing of the payer's assets in conferring the relevant benefit might have been offset to some degree by a compensating adjustment to the price of his product. It is interesting to note that in Sebel Products Ltd. v. Commissioners of Customs and Excise[166] no claim was in fact made for recovery in respect of sales where the taxpayer had irretrievably "passed on" the purchase tax but the issue is whether the fact that the burden of a charge has been passed on should as a matter of law preclude recovery to avoid a "windfall" for the payer.

3.82   It may be argued that as a matter of principle such a defence should not be allowed since the net result is likely to be the enrichment of the administration which has acted unlawfully. The ultimate burden of the unlawful charge will be borne by the purchasers of the product who are unlikely to sue for the additional amount paid, and it is argued that it is better that any net "windfall" should

---

166.   [1949] 1 All E.R. 729, 730; paras. 2.10, 3.52 above. (Vaisey J's statement of the facts is omitted from [1949] 1 Ch. 409).

go to the payer rather than the authority which has acted unlawfully.

3.83   As far as the general law of restitution is concerned a claim may be available even though a benefit conferred by the plaintiff has not actually caused him any loss[167].   It may be argued that it is a defence to show that the plaintiff has suffered no loss: although the recipient's interest in the security of his receipt must give way to that of the plaintiff when the plaintiff has suffered loss, it should be protected where no such loss has occurred.[168] The question of whether recovery should be denied where the burden of the invalid charge has been passed on was considered in Air Canada v. British Columbia.[169]   La Forest J., with whom Lamer and L'Heureux Dube JJ. agreed, considered that "passing on" should be a defence, stating that "the law of restitution is not intended to provide windfalls to plaintiffs who have suffered no loss".   Wilson J. on the other hand, thought that it should not be a defence: it was not legitimate to retain a payment made pursuant to an unconstitutional statute.   In the United Kingdom in the case of the recovery of V.A.T., car tax, and excise duty the legislation makes it a defence that the payer would be "unjustly enriched" if he

---

167.   Mason v. New South Wales (1959) 102 C.L.R. 108. The point was discussed by Windeyer J. (p.146) who appeared to state that absence of loss to the plaintiff is never a defence; but an alternative interpretation may be that the Court's refusal to apply the defence was based on the fact that the claim was founded on duress, i.e. wrongful conduct by the payee.

168.   This assumes no change of position by the payee; where there is such a change the balance may differ. See paras. 3.77-3.78 above.

169.   [1989] S.C.R. 1161 (Supreme Court of Canada).

recovered the payment. The European Court has held that national states may provide for such a defence.[170] However, Community law appears to require that the burden of proving that the payer would be enriched by allowing recovery must rest with the levying authority so as to satisfy the requirement that remedies provided are not "impossible in practice or excessively difficult" to exercise.[171]

3.84   There are also practical objections to the defence. It would be difficult to determine the precise extent to which the charge has in fact been passed on. In addition, the increase in price may have lead to a decrease in demand so as to negate any "windfall" element.[172] One way of meeting the practical difficulties would be to require the authority to prove that the amount of the charge has been added to the price, and to require the payer then to prove by way of rebuttal the effect which this increase has had on sales. However, where Community law applies this approach may not be possible.

3.85   In principle there would appear to be no reason why such a defence should not apply to cases where the authority can prove on the balance of probabilities that the payer would be unjustly enriched because the charge has been passed on. The views of consultees on the general issue of a "passing on" defence are invited.

---

170.   Case 68/79 Hans Just I/S v. Danish Ministry for Fiscal Affairs [1980] E.C.R. 501.

171.   Case 199/82 Amministrazione delle Finanze dello Stato v. SpA San Giorgio [1983] E.C.R. 3595.

172.   On these difficulties see Rudden and Bishop, "Gritz and Quellmehl: Pass it on" (1981) 6 E.L.Rev. 243.

(d)   The Problem of Technical Invalidity

3.86   A charge may be levied which is "technically" invalid in the sense that had the government acted lawfully a charge of the same amount would have been levied anyway. For instance, a charge may be levied in breach of a duty to consult or to take account of a particular factor but is subsequently levied following consultation or taking account of the factor.   One possible approach is for the courts to attempt to assess what the position would have been apart from the breach and to take this into account in determining the scope of liability.   Thus, in the above example, resolving all doubts in favour of the citizen, if the charge would have been imposed in any event recovery should not be allowed.   However, the question of what would have happened is a difficult one, and in other public law contexts in which it has been considered, it has been criticised.   But it is suggested this possibility ought to be taken into account where the position is clear for example, where a similar charge has in fact subsequently been lawfully imposed.[173]   This result could be achieved through a requirement that there should be no recovery where the government can prove that the payer has suffered no loss as a result of the payment.

---

173.   This occurred in Air Canada v. British Columbia [1989] 1 S.C.R. 1161 in which the government had subsequently passed legislation imposing a different tax of effectively the same amount, but framed in such a way that it was valid. The issue of recovery where the invalidity is purely technical was not, however, discussed.   It should be noted that in this case the tax had in fact been made retrospective and this provided another reason for the decision.

5. THE SCOPE OF THE GENERAL RESTITUTIONARY PRINCIPLE

(a) To which Bodies and Functions Should it Apply

3.87   The principle recently formulated by the majority in Woolwich Equitable Building Society v. I.R.C. recognises a general public law right to restitution in the case of a payment made in response to an ultra vires levy.   What is unclear is precisely to what bodies and types of payments the principle should apply.   In defining what cases fall within the public law sphere Glidewell L.J. referred to where "the Defendant is an instrument or officer of central or local government, exercising a power to require payment of a tax, customs duty, licence fee or similar impost" in which case "[t]he payment is required under what purports to be a statutory power enabling the Defendant to claim such a payment, sometimes in return for a licence, in other cases simply as part of a general power to levy a tax or customs duty".   Butler-Sloss L.J. categorised as coming within "public law" the situation where "someone with actual or ostensible authority to require payment in respect of tax, duty, licence fee or other payment on behalf of central or local government makes the demand for payment".

3.88   The position of utilities such as the gas, water and electricity companies, and other corporations incorporated under the Companies Acts, which are given statutory, and hence limited, power to levy charges for the provision of goods or services is unclear.   Although unauthorised charges are not in the nature of a tax or licence fee, they might be regarded as subject to public law principles.[174]   One approach is to provide in general

---

174.   See, e.g., Foster v. British Gas plc [1991] 2 W.L.R. 1075, in which the European Court and the House of Lords treated a corporation as part of the state for the purposes of the doctrine of direct

terms that the principle should apply to all payments levied in breach of public law, and to leave it to the courts to define what is meant by public law. Alternatively, the position of utilities and other corporations referred to above could be addressed specifically.

3.89   Our provisional view is that the general restitutionary principle set out in Woolwich should apply in the context of any levy in breach of public law or community law and any levy purportedly made under statutory authority to a utility or corporation which is in fact unauthorised. However, we would welcome comments on the appropriate scope of the principle.

(b)   Requirement of an Invalid Demand?

3.90   Whatever the scope of the rule adopted we do not consider that anything should turn on the existence or otherwise of an actual demand for payment: the right to recover should be based simply on the fact that there is no authority to levy such a payment. Recovery should even be allowed in those rare cases where the payer himself has taken the initiative in making the payment. We consider that any other rule would create too many difficulties. Clearly it should not be necessary that an express demand for payment should be made in each case and it might be difficult to distinguish a payment made in response to an implied demand, or an "expectation" of payment generated by

---

174.   Continued
        effect as it was a body which was made responsible,
        pursuant to a measure adopted by the state, for
        providing a public service under the control of the
        state and had, for that purpose, special powers
        beyond those which resulted from the normal rules
        applicable in relations between individuals.

the authority, from a payment on the initiative of the payer. The existing statutory rights of recovery are framed in these terms: for example section 24 of the Finance Act 1989 allows recovery where a person has paid an amount "by way of value added tax which was not tax due." A similar formula could be used in a general recovery provision.

6. EXCLUSIVE NATURE OF THE RULE

3.91   Finally, while recognising the problems of definition, we believe that, as in the case of section 24 of the Finance Act 1989,[175] any statutory right of recovery should be the exclusive method of recovery available in respect of ultra vires receipts. It would be unnecessary to resort to the common law as far as the substantive grounds of recovery are concerned, since the statutory right of recovery is to be a general one. As far as limitations on recovery, such as a shorter limitation period or the "passing on" defence, are concerned, it appears contrary to principle that a litigant should be able to circumvent these by bringing an action under the common law. We invite the views of consultees on this issue.

---

175.   See para. 3.21 above.

PART IV: CLAIMS BY PUBLIC BODIES

1. THE CURRENT LAW

a) Recovery under the Common Law

4.1   The distinct position of public authorities has been recognised by the common law, which has applied a special rule to permit them to recover payments made beyond their statutory authority. In Auckland Harbour Board v. R. Viscount Haldane stated that

> "Any payment out of the consolidated fund made without Parliamentary authority is simply illegal and ultra vires and may be recovered by the Government if it can... be traced."[1]

4.2   The principle was stated to be wider than that which applies between citizens and appears to allow recovery simply because the payment was ultra vires. The payment may be recovered although under a mistake of law, and this is thus one further qualification to the general mistake of law rule.   Lord Haldane's statement suggests, however, that it is not necessary that the payment be made as a result of mistake for it to be recoverable.[2] He appears to limit the principle to payments made from the Consolidated Fund, but such a limitation appears anomalous. The rule is said to be based on public policy; namely the protection of public funds from unlawful dissipation.   This rationale suggests that it probably ought to apply to all ultra vires payments made by government.

---

1.   [1924] A.C. 318, 327.

2.   See also Commonwealth of Australia v. Crothall Hospital Services (Aust) Ltd.   (1981) 36 A.L.R. 567; Sandvik Australia Pty. Ltd. v. Commonwealth of Australia (1989) 89 A.L.R. 213.

4.3   The Supreme Court of Victoria in _Commonwealth_ v.
Burns held that the government cannot be estopped from
claiming repayment: "a party cannot be assumed by the
doctrine of estoppel to have lawfully done that which the
law says that he shall not do".[3]   English law also
recognises the limitations of estoppel in public law[4]
although in certain situations a public body may be estopped
by a representation made by it even where the representation
is ultra vires.[5]   If this approach were to be extended to
ultra vires payments, a narrow defence might be developed.
As a defence of change of position has only recently been
recognised in England, its application in this situation has
not been considered although the policy considerations
involved are similar to those concerning estoppel.

4.4   The question whether a citizen might raise as a
defence that the government has made a submission to an
honest claim does not appear to have been considered.

(b)   Recovery under Statute

4.5   The recovery of welfare benefits, including social
security benefit, child benefit, income support, family
credit and certain payments from the Social Fund,[6] is dealt
with by section 53 of the Social Security Act 1986 and

---

3.   [1971] V.R. 825, 830.

4.   See Craig, Administrative Law (2nd ed., 1989), Ch. 16.

5.   Western Fish Products Ltd v. Penwith D.C. [1981] 2 All
      ER 204.   See generally Craig, Administrative Law, op
      cit, pp.474-6 and note also the protection of
      "legitimate expectations".

6.   As specified in Social Security Act 1986, section
      53(10).

the relevant regulations.[7] By these provisions overpayments by the government (including those made under mistake of law) are only recoverable if caused by a claimant's misrepresentation or failure to disclose a material fact.[8] However, non-recoverable payments may be offset against other benefits payable.[9] This would include payments made as a result of mistake of law.

(c)   The Requirements of European Community Law

(i)   Payments Unlawfully Made under Community Provisions

4.6   A number of schemes concerned with agricultural products, administered by member states on behalf of the Community, provide for subsidies and grants to be paid from Community resources. Payments made under such schemes may infringe Community law, as in the case of a discriminatory subsidy, or be based on an erroneous interpretation of Community legislation, as where a subsidy is given to a party which is not entitled to it. Any action for recovery must be brought against the payee in national courts in accordance with national law and procedure.[10]

---

7. Social Security (Payments on account, Overpayments and Recovery) Regulations 1988, S.I. 1988 No. 664, on which see R v. Secretary of State for Social Security, Ex p. Britnell [1991] 1 W.L.R. 198.

8. Social Security Act 1986, section 53(1). S.I. 1988 No. 664, reg. 5. See Secretary of State for Social Security v. Tunnicliffe, [1991] 2 All E.R. 712.

9. S.I. 1988 No. 664, reg. 5.

10. Case 265/78 H. Ferwerda B.V. v. Produktschap voor Vee en Vlees [1980] E.C.R. 617; Case 54/81 Firma Wilhelm Fromme v. Bundesanstalt [1982] E.C.R. 1449; Cases 205-215/82 Deutsche Milchkontor v. Germany [1983] E.C.R. 2633.

4.7   This basic principle is qualified by Community legislation and other rules of Community law. Member States are under a general obligation to provide for the recovery of agricultural subsidies,[11] and the remedy must comply with the principle of effectiveness. In the absence of specific legislation it seems that the same requirement would arise from general principles of Community law to uphold the policies behind the Community law restrictions.[12] However, substantial limitations on recovery are permissible and may indeed be required by Community law to protect the recipient's legitimate expectations in the security of his receipt.[13]   Thus, recovery may be limited by a short limitation period, by a defence of change of position or where there has been no "fault" on the part of the payee.[14] In this context any national remedy must also comply with the principle of non-discrimination; the remedy must be neither more nor less favourable than that which applies to comparable domestic claims.[15]

[11.] Council Regulation 29/70 Article 8(1).

[12.] In Ferwerda, it is clear that the court considered the same principles would apply where there was no relevant legislative provision.

[13.] See the statement in Case 11/76 Netherlands v. Commission, [1979] E.C.R. 245, 278, suggesting that it may not be possible under Community law to recover sums paid in error, thus considerably reducing the impact of the regulation.

[14.] See the cases cited above, para. 4.6, note 10.

[15.] H. Ferwerda B.V. v. Produktschap voor Vee en Vlees [1980] E.C.R. 617. Deutsche Milchkontor v. Germany [1983] E.C.R. 2633 concerned the permissibility of provisions which restricted the right of the administration to recover. Firma Wilhelm Fromme v. Bundesanstalt [1982] E.C.R. 1449 concerned the stringency of the burden on the recipient - here the question of whether interest could be demanded from the recipient.

(ii)   Unlawful State Aids[16]

4.8   "State aids", that is, aid given by the authorities in member states from their own resources, may also raise restitutionary problems.[17]   An aid payment without prior notification to the Commission or which is paid during the period of "review" by the Commission, or which, following such review, is found incompatible with the common market, will be unlawful.[18]

4.9   Action to recover an unlawful payment must be brought in national courts and will be determined according to national law and procedure,[19] but subject to the principles of effectiveness and non-discrimination.   There may be no restrictions on recovery where the payee has not got a legitimate expectation that the payments are lawful and in several cases on state aids it has been held that there is no such expectation.[20]   It seems unlikely that an unlawful state aid will arise as a consequence of a mistake of law as opposed to a mistake of fact or a deliberate breach of Community rules.

---

16. See generally Wyatt and Dashwood, The Substantive Law of the EEC (2nd ed., 1987) Ch. 17.

17. For an explanation of the kind of payments falling within these provisions see Wyatt and Dashwood, op. cit, pp. 453-459.

18. E.C. Treaty, Arts. 92, 93; Case C-5/89 Commission of the European Communities v. Federal Republic of Germany, The Times, 8 November 1990.

19. Art. 93.   See Wyatt and Dashwood, op. cit., pp.464-469.

20. Case C-5/89, Commission of the European Communities v. Federal Republic of Germany, The Times, 8 November 1990.   The case concerned a state aid which was unlawful for failure to notify the Commission at all.   No doubt the same principles would apply to aids which are unlawful for the other reasons mentioned above.

2. EVALUATION OF THE LAW

(a) Justification for the General Rule

4.10   Insofar as the common law rule applicable to payments by public authorities allows the recovery of payments made under mistake of law, in this context as in general,[21] it is supportable on the basis of the prevention of unjust enrichment. The wider aspect of the rule, which probably allows recovery even where there is no mistake by the authority, has been justified by the public policy against the unlawful dissipation of public funds.

(b)   Should there be Reform?

4.11   There seem to be three alternatives. One is to leave the current rule unchanged and to accept ultra vires or some similar concept as the basis for recovery. The second is to assimilate the law to the ordinary private law, so that recovery would require proof of a recognised ground for restitution. The third is to make a more radical change to the current law by limiting the right of recovery to situations where the payee is in some way at fault.

(i)   Retention of the Existing Rule

4.12   The justification for the existing rule is the need to protect public funds. The significance of the difference between this and the private law approach based on mistake may depend largely on the width of the common law doctrine

---

21. See para. 2.24 above.

of mistake, and also on the availability of the defences of compromise and submission to an honest claim.[22]

4.13   The Law Reform Commission of British Columbia favoured the retention of the common law principle of recovery.[23]   On this approach further development would be left to the common law.

(ii)   Application of the Ordinary Private Law

4.14   If the law were to be reformed along the lines provisionally suggested in Part II to allow recovery where there has been a mistake of law, recovery would be available in many of the cases now dealt with by the Auckland Harbour rule, although not where the authority knew the payment was not due.   It is difficult to see that the authority's interests should prevail where the paying officer believes the payment is invalid and it may be that a rule based on mistake would be more equitable.

(iii)   Limitation of the General Recovery Principle

4.15   The apparently more radical option would be to introduce a general rule which allows recovery only in very limited circumstances, for example where there is some kind of fault on the part of the recipient.   This would be similar to the statutory provisions on the recovery of certain welfare benefits outlined in paragraph 4.5 which would in substance remain unchanged.   The argument for such

---

22. See the discussion at paras. 3.65-3.69 above.

23. Report on the Recovery of Unauthorised Disbursements of Public Funds, LRC 48 (1980).

a reform would be the special responsibility of the authority to know the law and the fact that it is in the best position to avoid any mistakes. Such a rule might also be thought of as a simpler version of the change of position defence: since there will normally have been a change of position it is convenient to adopt an "irrebuttable presumption" to this effect to avoid any potentially complex disputes. It may also be noted that, as explained in paragraph 4.7, Community law may require that in certain circumstances recovery of overpayments should be restricted or refused to protect a payee's legitimate expectations.

4.16   However, the question of recovery of ultra vires payments may arise in a wide variety of fact situations and it does not necessarily follow that a rule denying recovery should apply in every case. The arguments mentioned above reflect the considerations which are currently taken into account by the courts in applying the principles of estoppel, and in particular when to imply a representation.[24]   The application of estoppel to ultra vires payments might achieve a similar result to the enactment of a special statutory rule which precludes recovery in cases where there has been reliance on the payment, and estoppel might be a better way of dealing with the matter. The courts would have flexibility to tailor the solution to the particular context. Furthermore, incidental questions such as the effect of the fault of the payee are probably better worked out on a case by case basis as they arise.

[24.] See Birks, "The Recovery of Carelessly Mistaken Payments" [1972] C.L.P. 179.

4.17   We have not formed a view as to which of these
approaches would be the better one and invite comment on
these matters.

(iv)   Defences

Change of Position

4.18   It is our provisional view that the defence of
change of position should be available in an action for the
recovery of an overpayment made by a public authority,
whether this is based on mistake or on ultra vires: the
interest in the lawful expenditure of public funds does not
seem to us to be sufficient to override the interest of the
payee who has changed his position in reliance on the
receipt of the payment. This was also the view of the Law
Reform Commission of British Columbia[25] and the Law Reform
Committee of South Australia.[26]

4.19   It may also be asked whether the defence should be
available where the right of recovery is given under a
specific statute. Where a claim is brought under statute it
might be argued that the defence should be inapplicable in
the absence of a specific provision. Without such a
provision any case would be likely to produce complex
arguments regarding the relationship of the specific
statutory provision to the general defence and to any
general right of recovery existing outside the statute. In

---

25. LRC 48 (1980), p.12.   This led to the enactment of
     section 67(1) of the Financial Administration Act 1981.

26. Report Relating to the Irrecoverability of Benefits
     Obtained by Reason of Mistake of Law (84th Report, 1984)
     pp. 32-33.

principle, however, there is a case for making the defence available. We invite the views of consultees on this question. One way of handling the issue would be to provide that the "change of position defence" apply generally to statutory rights of recovery and to require specific exclusion of the defence where appropriate (for example in claims against public authorities).

Estoppel

4.20   As indicated in para. 4.3 above, the defence of estoppel probably does not apply in an action to recover an ultra vires payment. This may not be such a serious problem since in cases where the recipient has acted in reliance on the payment the defence of change of position may cover the situation. However, it is relevant to consider whether the estoppel defence should, in principle, be available also.

4.21   We incline to the view that the fact that a payment made is ultra vires does not provide a very solid reason for giving less protection to a party's interest than he would receive were this not the case, and that a good argument can be made for allowing the estoppel doctrine to operate in the absence of a demonstrated overriding public interest. However, we recognise that wider issues are raised by the operation of estoppel where a public authority has acted ultra vires and defer forming a view until we receive the views of consultees.

PART V : CONCLUSION AND SUMMARY OF CONSULTATION ISSUES

5.1   In this paper we have considered the general rule
that payments made under a mistake of law are irrecoverable
and the position of ultra vires payments to and by public
authorities.   We have canvassed a number of possible reforms
and have considered their implications.   The case for reform
is based on the fact that it is unjust that as between the
parties the payee should be able to retain a payment
received at the expense of the payer because of the payer's
mistake.   This basic principle is recognised in the law
relating to payments made as a result of a mistake of fact.
The different treatment given to mistakes of law and
mistakes of fact is inconsistent and arbitrary, and these
features of the law are exacerbated by the development of
many exceptions to the mistake of law rule.   There have,
moreover, been important statutory modifications of the
rule.   Different treatment of apparently similar cases may
be justified if there are strong pragmatic grounds, but here
the arguments appear unconvincing.   The uncertainty and
complexity of the present law and the fact that the general
restitutionary principle enunciated in <u>Woolwich Equitable
Building Society</u> v. <u>I.R.C.</u>[1] does not apply to payments made
under a mistake of law also suggest that reform is
desirable.   We have expressed a provisional view on a number
of issues.   These views are, of course, subject to what is
said in response to this paper.

5.2   **Our provisional conclusions on the main issues are
as follows:**

        (a)   there is a case for abolishing the rule
        precluding the recovery of payments made as a

---

[1].   The Times, 27 May 1991.

133

result of a mistake of law so as to permit recovery in the same way that it is currently allowed where the payment is made under a mistake of fact (paragraphs 2.36-2.37 above),

(b) if there is to be reform of the mistake of law rule as outlined above, it is important that claims for restitution on this ground should be subject to the newly recognised defence of change of position which should, however, be left to be developed by the common law (paragraphs 2.66-2.79 above),

(c) in the case of payments made to a public authority existing statutory rights of recovery should be rationalised, there should be a general right to recover which should not be confined to cases involving mistake but should, subject to special defences (summarised at paragraphs 3.65-3.86 above), in addition extend to all payments made pursuant to a demand made in breach of public law (including those in breach of EC law) (paragraphs 3.60-3.64 above), whether made under statutory or common law powers or levied in excess of statutory authority (paragraphs 3.87-3.88 above) and to all other payments made but not otherwise due because of a breach of public law (3.90 above),

(d) in the case of ultra vires payments made by a public authority, the public interest in ensuring that public funds are only used for lawful expenditure does not justify granting recovery in all circumstances (paragraphs 4.10-4.22 above).

Consultees' views are invited on each of these conclusions which we emphasise are only provisional. We are particularly anxious that any arguments we have overlooked or undervalued or any practical problems that have not been properly dealt with are brought to our attention.

5.3   If reform on the lines envisaged in paragraph 5.2 is to take place, its precise shape will depend on the answers to a number of further questions and we also invite comments on these matters.

5.4   **Provisional conclusion (a): abolition of the rule precluding recovery of payments made under a mistake of law**

> (i)   If reform of the mistake of law rule is to be by analogy to mistake of fact, what approach should be followed?   In particular should the courts be directed to grant recovery whenever recovery would be granted were the mistake one of fact (paragraphs 2.45-2.52 above)?

> (ii)   How should the problem of changes in the understanding of the law be dealt with (paragraphs 2.57-2.65 above)?

> (iii)   Are there any further issues relating to the general law of mistake which should be specifically considered?

5.5   **Provisional conclusion (b): the defence of change of position**

> (i)   Should development of the defence be left to the common law (paragraphs 2.70-2.78 above)?   If not;

(ii)   What should be the scope of the defence
(i.e. the type of reliance required, the relevance
of fault and, the relationship of the defence to
estoppel: paragraphs 2.70-2.73 above)?

(iii)   Should the defence be available in
respect of statutory actions for restitution
(paragraph 2.79 above)? In particular, in the case
of payments to or by a public authority, should the
defence be available for all payments made but not
lawfully due (paragraphs 3.77-3.78 and 4.18-4.19
above)?

5.6   **Provisional conclusion (c): recognition of a right
to restitutionary relief governing payments made pursuant to
an invalid demand by a public authority or where payment is
not otherwise due because of a breach of public law**

(i)   To what bodies and type of payment such a
right should apply (paragraphs 3.87-3.90 above)?

(ii)   Should a public authority have power to
make a binding compromise or settlement in respect
of such a demand?

(iii)   Should such a right deal with the problem
of disruption of public finances by precluding
recovery of payments made in accordance with
general practice or claims made after the
determination of the payment's invalidity, allowing
for the defence of change of position, applying
shorter limitation periods, introducing a defence
of "passing on" or by other means (paragraphs
3.65-3.86 above)?

5.7   **Provisional conclusion (d): modification of the rule permitting a public authority to recover all ultra vires payments**

> Should recovery be permitted (i) only where there has been some fault on the part of the recipient or, (ii) in all cases but subject to defences such as change of position or estoppel (paragraphs 4.15-4.21)?

Printed in the United Kingdom by HMSO, Edinburgh Press
Dd 0293224 C17 7/91 (291572)